TURKEY

SYRIA

RHODES

LEBANON

CYPRUS

MEDITERRANEAN
SEA

ISRAEL

EGYPT

CYPRUS

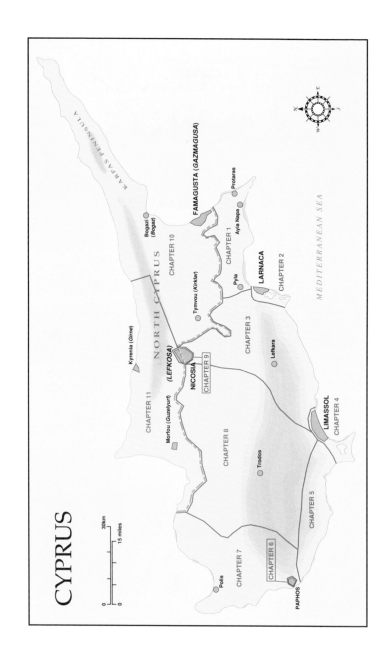

30km
15 miles

N

MEDITERRANEAN SEA

KARPAS PENINSULA

NORTH CYPRUS

CHAPTER 11

CHAPTER 10

CHAPTER 8

CHAPTER 9

CHAPTER 7

CHAPTER 6

CHAPTER 5

CHAPTER 4

CHAPTER 3

CHAPTER 2

CHAPTER 1

Kyrenia (Girne)

Morfou (Guzelyurt)

Trodos

Lefkara

Tymvou (Kirklar)

Bogazi (Bogaz)

Pyla

Ayia Napa

Protaras

NICOSIA (LEFKOSA)

FAMAGUSTA (GAZMAGUSA)

LARNACA

LIMASSOL

PAPHOS

Polis

VISITOR'S GUIDE
CYPRUS

Fiona Bulmer

MPC
HUNTER

Published by:
Moorland Publishing Co Ltd,
Moor Farm Road West,
Ashbourne,
Derbyshire DE6 1HD
England

ISBN 0 86190 471 0

Published in the USA by:
Hunter Publishing Inc,
300 Raritan Center Parkway,
CN 94, Edison, NJ 08818

ISBN 1 55650 551 5 (USA)

British Library Cataloguing in
Publication Data:
A catalogue record for this book is
available from the British Library.

Colour origination by:
P & W Graphics Pte Ltd, Singapore

Printed in the UK by:
Bath Press Colourbooks

Cover photograph: Ayia Napa
(*International Photobank*)

Illustrations have been supplied as
follows: Fiona Bulmer pages 16, 27,
31 lower, 35 top, 58, 87, 110, 131
top, 135, lower; Robert Bulmer
pages 11 lower, 31 top, 35 lower,
38, 39, 51, 79 top, 95 lower, 98
lower, 99 top, 103, 115, 127, 131
lower, 135 top, 147, 155, 159; G.
Irving page 118; MPC Picture
Collection pages 11 top, 18, 66, 67,
71, 74, 75, 79 lower, 82, 83, 84, 94,
95 top, 98 top, 99 lower, 119, 122

Acknowledgements
The author would like to thank
Robert and Mary Bulmer for their
help in the research and writing of
this book.

The Author
Fiona Bulmer has long-standing
ties with Cyprus, as she grew up
on the island and lived there for
seven years. She has travelled
widely throughout Cyprus, knows
the island well and has a keen
interest in Cypriot history and
culture. She has also written the
Visitor's Guide to Crete which has
been widely acclaimed and
recommended by readers.

MPC Production Team
Editorial and Design: John Robey
Cartography: Alastair Morrison

CONTENTS

Key to Symbols Used in Text Margin and on Maps

⌂	Church/Monastery/ Mosque	☀	Other place of interest
♜	Castle	🌲	Beautiful view/Scenery/ Natural phenomenon
Π	Archaeological Site	🚶	Recommended walk
🏛	Museum/Art gallery	🦌	Animal interest
⊞	Building of interest	🦆	Birdlife

Key to Maps

═══	Motorway	⬭	City
━━━	Main Road	●	Town /Village
═══	Secondary Road		River/Lake
═══	Minor Road	-----	National Boundary

How To Use This Guide

This MPC Visitor's Guide has been designed to be as easy to use as possible. Each chapter covers a region or itinerary in a natural progression which gives all the background information to help you enjoy your visit. MPC's distinctive margin symbols, the important places printed in bold, and a comprehensive index enable the reader to find the most interesting places to visit with ease. At the end of each chapter an Additional Information section gives specific details such as addresses and opening times, making this guide a complete sightseeing companion. At the back of the guide the Fact File, arranged in alphabetical order, gives practical information and useful tips to help you plan your holiday — before you go and while you are there. The maps of each region show the main towns, villages, roads and places of interest, but are not designed as route maps and motorists should always use a good recommended road atlas.

INTRODUCTION

Cyprus is a modernised, westernised place; sixty years of British rule have made sure of that, the people drive on the left and almost everyone speaks English. This sense of familiarity combined with the sun, sand and sea make it an increasingly popular holiday destination. Of course the westernisation is only skin deep; the culture is fundamentally Mediterranean and at times Byzantine. They may drive on the left but cannot be relied upon to stop at red lights. Cypriots may work in modern office blocks but do business in quite a different way, they are more relaxed but perhaps less reliable. And the sun, sand and sea are only part of the picture; the mountains, the villages, and the ancient sites will fill in much more.

The island lies at the far eastern end of the Mediterranean and has been able to keep the recent conflicts of the Middle East at arms length, serving as a safe haven for refugees, foreign correspondents and resting military. However, its own internal conflict has rumbled on for 400 years; that of Greeks versus Turks which led to the division of the island. Although the current dispute has all the paraphernalia of a modern conflict — barbed wire and United Nations troops — it is essentially an ancient conflict and talk of the Turkish invasion in history books may not always refer to that of 1974 but that of 1570, both of which transformed the island's history.

Cyprus is the third largest island in the Mediterranean, 150 miles long (240km) and 60 miles (95km) wide with an area of 3,584 square miles (9,282 square km), a mere 7 per cent of the size of England. That already insubstantial size is reduced further by the division of the island. The southern part, the Greek Cypriot area, covers 60 per cent of the territory and is that which most tourists will see. The northern Turkish sector, still unrecognised by the international community, is much less tourist oriented, but even Greek Cypriots may admit that it has some of the best scenery.

Once in the island this division does not make a great deal of practical difference to the visitor except for those who want to see the whole island. Transfer from the northern side to the southern side is impossible and the reverse journey is only allowed for a day through the checkpoint at Nicosia.

The island's regions offer contrasting views and landscapes. Eastern Cyprus is flat; transformed into fine agricultural land through extensive irrigation of its fertile red soil. Cyprus potatoes, found in shops in Britain come from this part of the island. The steel windmills which are such a characteristic part of the landscape are irrigation pumps and are essential to the fertility of the region.

It is here that the best beaches have been developed for the tourists. Out at Ayia Napa, at the far eastern end of the island, is perhaps the main beach resort and has been developed very much as a substitute for Famagusta, the occupied city which can be seen shimmering in the distance from certain roads in the far east of the island.

In this region too is the British Sovereign Base of Dhekalia with its green fields and red brick houses which serve as a reminder of the continuing links with Britain. The sovereign bases were granted to Britain under the Independence agreement and are much sought after postings for British soldiers. They are of considerable strategic importance, especially given the volatile nature of the Middle East.

The Central Plain, also known as the Mesaoria, is green and vibrant in spring but in summer becomes a dusty, barren area with Nicosia, the island's capital, at its centre. Nicosia is a divided city and has the only point at which one can cross from one side of the island to the other. The old city is enclosed by its Venetian walls while the wide avenues of the modern city radiate beyond.

The Troodos mountains are very high and offer ideal landscapes for walkers and in winter for skiers. A hardy visitor could spend the morning on the beach and the afternoon on the ski slopes. The mountains are full of Byzantine churches which have distinctive steep pitched roofs and contain many fine collections of wall paintings which illustrate the whole of the New Testament. The surrounding scenery is often spectacular, set with villages which tumble down the hillside in their typical ramshackle way. When the heat of the plain becomes too oppressive, the mountains offer a freshness and verdant landscape which is particularly attractive.

The far west of the island, beyond Paphos, is as yet quiet. Its lack of roads and general inaccessibility have meant the area remained isolated but the building of the international airport at Paphos has brought many more visitors to this end of the island and developers are eyeing some of the more remote and unspoiled parts of the area.

The north of the island offers a different kind of scenery; the Kyrenia mountains, (*Besparmak* hills in Turkish), are lower than the Troodos but their craggy outlines overlooking the sea are just as impressive. Kyrenia (*Girne*) sits on the coast below the hills set around a distinctive horsehoe harbour. To the west is Morphou Bay (*Guzelyurt Bay*), which is a fertile area irrigated by the melting, mountain snow and well known for its citrus production. To the east, the coast stretches up to the 'panhandle', the remote Karpas which has few inhabitants, some in Greek enclaves. Famagusta (*Gazimagusa*), to the south, is the most striking reminder of the island's troubled past. The modern city has stood empty since the 1974 invasion and only the military can enter. The old town, which was always Turkish, does however remain accessible and, surrounded by its Venetian city walls, is one of the most impressive cities of its kind in the Mediterranean.

The archaeological sites of Cyprus cannot be ignored, even by the most philistine of visitors. *Kourion* (*Curium*), on the south coast is one of the most spectacular, with its theatre high on the cliff overlooking the sea, and which is still used today for theatrical perfomances. The sites of Nea Paphos spill all around the town from the Tombs of the Kings to the pillar at which St Paul was allegedly whipped. *Salamis*, in the Turkish part of the island, has a much photographed gymnasium and there are many other more minor sites scattered around the island.

Landscape and Resources

The island has an area of 3,584 square miles (9,282 square km) and is strategically located at the far eastern end of the Mediterranean. To a certain extent it is suprising that it should have become so dominated by Greek culture as Syria is only 60 miles (95km) away and Turkey even closer at 43 miles (69km) whereas it is 270 miles (432km) from Rhodes and 500 miles (800km) from Piraeus.

The island, 150 miles (240km) long by 60 miles (95km) at its widest, is characterised by a central plain, bounded by two mountain ranges. The 480 miles (768km) of coast varies from rocky stretches to long sandy beaches with natural deep water harbours at Limassol and Famagusta.

The Troodos mountain range is more than 6,000ft (1,826m) high and was formed from volcanic rock, which is now covered in pine and oak forests. The Kyrenia range reaches a height of 3,443ft (1,046m) and was created by shifts in the northern continental plates. It is made mainly of limestone.

The island's name probably originates from the Greek word for copper and Cyprus has considerable mineral resources of copper, iron and asbestos. Copper has been mined here since 3,000BC and was one of the island's major exports. Even in very early times there were well defined passes across the mountains and trails down to the harbours, from where the ore was shipped abroad. These days mineral deposits are dwindling, although asbestos is still mined in the Troodos mountains.

The island has frequently been subject to earthquakes, although the last major one occurred fifty years ago. The southern and eastern coasts have suffered particularly badly over the years and historic sites such as *Alasia*, *Salamis* and *Kition* were all damaged by early quakes.

The island used to be covered in forests but these were cut down; first to build ships for the Persian army and Alexander the Great and later to provide grazing land. Forests are now visible only in the Troodos range where the Forestry Commission has embarked on extensive reafforestation projects with the result that 18 per cent of the island is now covered in trees.

In the Middle Ages the main exports were sugar and cotton and Cyprus was a major trading nation. Later salt from the lakes near Akrotiri and Larnaca was added to the list of Cypriot products. Nowadays tourism and agriculture are the mainstays of the Cypriot economy. The influence of agriculture is declining, in 1975 it contributed 15 per cent of GDP, today this has been halved to 7.5 per cent.

Grapes are the main product with 212,000 tons produced each year from the 18 per cent of the land devoted to vineyards. Citrus fruits and vegetables, especially potatoes, are the other significant crops, not to mention the ubiquitous olive trees. The main citrus groves used to be in the northern part of the island, but now they are also in the south, mainly in the Phassouri area near Limassol. The mountains are characterised by the fruit trees and in spring offer picturesque views of cherry and almond trees in blossom.

A good deal of the agricultural production in the mountains still takes place in a rather primitve way, with the donkey playing a central part where the landscape makes modern machinery less useful. However, fruit production on the plains is much more sophisticated and expanding into new products such as bananas, grown in plantations near Paphos.

It is however, tourism which dominates the economy. There were 1.3 million visitors in 1989 who provided CY£490 million in foreign currency earnings for the island.

Cyprus also claims to be the business centre of the Middle East and

Bananas, with their huge flowers, are now being grown around Paphos

Fields of wild flowers in the springtime

this is borne out by the number of foreign firms — 4,700 in 1988 — which are registered on the island. Britain, however is Cyprus's main trading partner, taking over 21 per cent of its exports in 1988.

Cyprus is clearly one of the most prosperous places in the eastern Mediterranean, having recovered spectacularly from the economic blows which occurred after the 1974 troubles. Unemployment reached 25 per cent in that period but now stands at only 2 per cent. The education, public health and in particular the housing systems coped well with the influx of refugees from the north and prosperity was soon regained. This affluence has allowed for several grand infrastructure projects to be completed, such as the new roads from the coast to Nicosia.

One area where grand projects are still needed is the water supply. Like many other Mediterranenan countries water shortages are common and houses are characterised by the large and ugly water tanks on their roofs. There are numerous irrigation schemes across the island mainly involving the construction of dams in the mountains and as a result much of the island has been made fertile, but the demands from the agricultural and tourist industries mean that the much talked about desalination plant may finally go ahead.

Plants and Animals

There is a profusion of flowers in spring in Cyprus, offering some spectacular views. Fields full of poppies are a common sight on the plains with wild gladioli in river beds. In March the acacia (mimosa) comes out in huge fluffy pollen covered buds, causing misery to hayfever sufferers, but is spectacular nonetheless. Anenomes are a common sight, the red ones are, according to legend, from the blood of Adonis whereas the white ones are the tears of Aphrodite on discovering Adonis dead. There are also 1,200 species of cyclamen growing wild.

In the mountains a whole array of miniature wild flowers are visible: crocuses, wild hyacinths and freesias. At the side of the roads are the long stemmed asphodel. There are numerous orchids including the bee orchid unique to Cyprus and a wide variety of herbs ranging from sage to lavender.

It is claimed that small elephants and hippopotami used to live on the island and skeletons of the latter have been found. The well known Cypriot animal is the moufflon, now a protected species which is found in reserves in the forests near Kykko monastery. It is a kind of sheep with distinctive curved horns and has become a strong symbol of Cyprus and used as a motif by the tourist office.

Donkeys are still the main working animals in the villages. On the farms there are few pigs and cows as the grazing land is not of high enough quality. There are, however, hundreds of sheep. These are fat tailed creatures which store fat in their tails to help them through the dry summer. Goats will also be seen roaming round and produce milk which is used to make halloumi cheese.

Cyprus once had many snakes but apparently St Helena brought cats to the island to hunt them and their numbers declined while the cats flourished. There is one poisonous snake, *vipera lebtina* (also known as the blunt nosed viper) with distinctive zigzag markings. It lives in remote parts of the mountains and is a particularly mean creature, as once it has caught it prey it pumps its jaws to ensure the venom fully penetrates the victim. However, more benevolent reptiles are much more common and the snakes' habit of lying soaking up the heat from roads means that the visitor is most likely to encounter the grisly remains of such ill-fated sunbathing rather than a live specimen.

Cyprus is on the migration path of a large number of birds and this can provide spectacular views for the ornithologists. However, bird watchers should avoid military areas where prominent signs prohibit photography and the use of binoculars. The most well known migrators are the flamingoes which gather on the salt lakes between February and October. The lakes also attracts a large number of other species including waders, sandpipers and terns.

In the mountains, falcons and vultures are often seen especially the griffon vulture. There are numerous warblers, including the Cyprus warblers endemic to the island. However, Cyprus is well known and much condemmned for its hunting of small songbirds which migrate here and then end up on the menu as a local delicacy.

In the sea there are many colourful fish and sea anenomes and provide plenty of opportunites for divers and snorkelling. The other famous residents of Cypriot waters are the turtles at Lara which are the subject of conservationists' concern in the light of increasing tourist development. The turtles are now protected in the fisheries department turtle hatchery where they come ashore to lay their eggs.

The climate is amenable to insects. Ants are everywhere as are mosquitoes, which are free of malaria, and in spring there is the chance to see a wide range of butterflies, including the swallowtail.

Art and Literature

Cyprus made little contribution to general Greek culture except through Zeno, who was born in Larnaca, and moved to Athens to found Stoicism. This philosophy said that as the gods were responsible for our suffering we should accept it without complaint.

Then in the Byzantine period prosperity came to the island and religious art became extremely significant and there are many fine painted churches.The paintings can be divided into chronological periods, Macedonians (867-1056), the Comneni (1081-1185) and the Palaeologi (1261-1453). They follow a particular pattern with a depiction of Christ pantokrator (ruler of the Universe) in the dome, surrounded by scenes from his life, ending with the crucifixion and anastasis (Christ's decent into Hades).

The Lusignan period concentrated on architecture and many fine public buildings were constructed across the island.

Overall the island has little of an international artistic or literary reputation, as its artistic tradition lies in folk ballads and the oral tradition and of course Greek dancing.

Nicosia sees a relatively large amount of modern theatre and cinema and there are productions in summer in the grand setting of the theatre at *Kourion* (*Curium*). Many of these productions are by the state subsidised Theatre of Cyprus Organisation.

Religion and Culture

Cyprus played a central role in Greek mythology as Aphrodite's birthplace. Aphrodite emerged from the sea at Petra tou Romiou and from then on Cyprus became a major centre of piligrimage, so that sanctuaries to Aphrodite can be found at several sites on the island. Aphrodite, as goddess of love, seems to have led a somewhat debauched life. She was given Hephaestus, a lame cobbler, as a husband but proceeded to have an affair with Ares. This led to a famous scene, recounted in the *Odyssey* when Hephaestus discovered them together and caught them in a net, summoning all the gods to come and laugh at them. Once released, Aphrodite went to 'Paphos in Cyprus where she has her precinct and fragrant altar'.

Undeterred by this experience Aphrodite took several other lovers, including Dionysos and Hermes. Adonis was her final lover and but he was killed by a boar while hunting near Idalion. The red flowers in the area are said to be the blood of Adonis while the white anenomes represent the tears of Aphrodite.

Pagan rituals and the cult of Aphrodite continued on the island until the Roman period. Christianity was then brought to Cyprus by St Paul and St Barnabas who, after some difficulties, including being tied to a pillar in Paphos, converted the Roman Governor and began its spread among the rest of the population.

During the Byzantine period Christianity became the official religion of the island and hundreds of churches were built. There was some conflict between the Orthodox and Latin churches during the

The Cypriots are welcoming to visitors

The traditional Cypriot bus is still to be seen, mainly catering for tourists

rule of the Lusignans. When the Turks invaded in 1570 many of the churches were converted into mosques. However, they allowed the archbishops to remain with considerable political power until 1831 when they suspected them of involvement in the Greek Independence movement and hanged several important bishops. Despite this the church survived and retained the loyalty of the population.

The Church came to prominence again in the fight against the British, supporting those who fought against them for independence. Indeed the figurehead of the independence struggle was Archbishop Makarios, also the head of the Church. The fact that he then became the first head of state after independence further underlines the central links between religion, politics and everyday life in Cyprus. However, this has diminished in recent years with the advent of a totally secular government.

Religion is still very important, though in a more subtle way, especially in the villages. The village priest will often be seen sitting in the local café and the festivals of the Greek Orthodox Church, especially Easter, are widely celebrated. Cypriots mark their saint's days much more than their birthdays and when the saint's day coincides with that of the village church there is likely to be a religious celebration involving the whole village.

Way of Life

Despite what seems to be a modern and westernised way of life the Greek Cypriots retain their distinctive culture which can sometimes surprise visitors. In most places entertainment still takes place in the café society and is exclusively male. In the villages the visitor will see old men in traditional baggy black trousers playing backgammon or in animated political discussion, their chairs spilling out into the road. More often than not the black-clad women of the village will be elsewhere, working in the fields.

The tourist office literature stresses the friendliness of the Cypriots and their generosity and for once it is no exaggeration. The Cypriots are especially friendly to visitors and are naturally gregarious. They will introduce themselves to perfect strangers and sit down and engage them in conversation. They may even invite you into their houses and ply you with bitter black coffee and sweet sticky cakes. The Turkish Cypriots tend to be quieter but equally hospitable.

Both communities have strong links with Britain, there are large numbers of Greeks and Turks now settled in London and they will often be seen on the flights to and from Cyprus. They are easily recognisable from the enormous amounts of hand baggage being transported back and forth: halloumi, melons, all the necessities of life which London apparently does not offer. This connection with England only increases their friendliness and with surprising naïvety they will often assume that a visitor from London is sure to know their cousin Yeorgios who lives in Barnet!

The Cypriot way of doing things, especially business, is much more relaxed than westerners are used to. Contracts and promises are there perhaps to be honoured, perhaps not, the undertaking to do something tomorrow is widespread. This can lead to frustration for those involved in such transactions. However, this relaxed attitude means that the shoemender will repair your shoes for nothing and the market trader will add an extra free orange to your bag.

Village life is still very important in Cypriot culture despite the extensive depopulation that has taken place over the past few decades. This means that the villages can have a ramshackle air and in the narrow streets chickens flee oncoming cars and black-clad peasants look as if this is the first motor vehicle they have ever seen. Even those who have moved away to the towns will come back to 'the village', and retain ties with it. Many will come by car, but the distinctive Cyprus bus still exists and can be seen careering down the mountains, usually overloaded. Although a relic from the past it is now increasingly being used as a tourist attraction.

The Cypriots are great family people. There is no better insight into Cypriot culture than a village wedding when all will gather, probably in the street, to celebrate and the visitor is likely to be welcomed. Afterwards a great feast will take place with the meat cooked in the large white *kleftiko* ovens.

Weddings in towns are more sober affairs but complete strangers are still likely to be invited, often through advertisements in the newspapers. The receptions take place in large hotels and the guests queue up to shake hands with the couple and to receive a piece of cake or sugared almonds.

The dowry system is still in operation in most of Cyprus and parents will spend most of their lives saving for a dowry for their daughter. The dowry is usually a house which is sometimes built on top of their own, which is the reason why so many Cypriot houses have a half-finshed look to them.

Food and Drink

Food and drink are an important part of Cypriot life as testified by the number of restaurants to be found both in Cyprus and in the extensive Cypriot communities abroad in which Cypriots find an outlet for their entrepreneurial skills.

Most meals will start with *mezedhes* (*meze*), a selection of appetisers

Stall selling nuts and sweets

Relaxing at a harbourside café

in small dishes which can be taken as a complete meal. They consist of dips such as *taramoslata* (fish roe paste), *tzatsiki* (yoghurt and cucumber) or *hoummous* (purée of chick peas). Olives are also a ubiquitous part of any meal.

For main courses: *kebab* is a simple and popular dish, pork or lamb cooked on skewers eaten with pitta bread, the original barbecue. These are known as *souvlakia*. Another meat dish is *kleftiko*, lamb cooked in a traditional slow oven. These white igloo-like constructions can still be seen in use especially in the mountain villages, while much older stone-built versions may also be found.

Moussaka is well known all over the world and contains layers of mince and aubergines, while *stifado* is a beef and tomato stew. All these dishes tend to be accompanied by Greek salad, tomato, cucumber and lettuce with fetta cheese.

Despite Cyprus being an island, fish is not plentiful and can be expensive. Swordfish and red mullet (*barbounia*) are the most widely available. Red snapper and squid (*kalamares*) are other possibilities.

Cypriots have a limited range of desserts which tend to be very sweet; *baklava* and *kadefi* are the most common in restaurants. It is also possible to have a cake in one of the many cake shops that can be found in the towns. They have a wide range of lavishly decorated cakes and can be taken away or eaten in the café usually with a black coffee (Greek or Turkish coffee depending on one's geographical situation) and a glass of water.

Turkish food is broadly similar although it may go under different names. *Sis kebap* is lamb roasted on a skewer and *doner kebap* roasted lamb or beef from a large turning spit from which thin slices are cut.

Cyprus has an extensive wine industry around Limassol. There is a wide selection of red and white wines, while locally made Keo and Carlsberg beers offer other alternatives. Brandy is a popular drink with the locals, it is produced on Cyprus and is often mixed with lemon juice or bitters to make brandy sour. Ouzo is an aniseed flavoured drink which is something of an acquired taste.

History

The tourist office claims Cyprus has 9,000 years of history, a period which keeps being extended as excavations proceed. Most of this has been turbulent, with the island coveted by all the changing powers in the region, all of which have left their mark even amidst the tourist centres; there is even an ancient tomb in the grounds of the Amamthus Bay hotel in Limassol. And, of course, Cyprus' more recent history cannot be avoided with the UN driving around in their white jeeps and the division of the island with barbed wire.

The first inhabitants of Cyprus date from around 7,000 BC, probably coming from the flourishing settlements in Anatolia or Syria. Indeed some archaeologists believe that there was probably some even earlier settlement, but no evidence has been found for this theory. The Neolithic settlements are found around the coasts, usually near a water supply. *Chorokoitia* is the best example, where people lived in distinctive beehive-shaped houses.

Around 3,000 BC copper began to be used for tools and organised communities began to grow up. There is evidence of a relatively sohpisticated culture and religious rites, especially burial rites. Many of the tombs have proved a rich source of artefacts, indicating that the dead were buried with their possessions.

The country seems to have been rich at this period, with agriculture the main occupation as many terracotta models have been found depicting ploughing scenes. The discovery of artefacts in Cyprus from the Minoan period in Crete suggest that there was extensive contact with the outside world.

The Late Bronze Age (1,600-1,050BC) saw increasing contact with other countries through trade and Mycenean settlers. Cyprus became an extremely important trading nation due mainly to its copper reserves and the metal was used to make fairly sophisticated tools ranging from tweezers to knives.

Although the island prospered, it does not seem to have been a peaceful time, with many of the settlements surrounded by thick walls and forts. There appears to have been much internal conflict between the east and west of the island. Despite this, more sophisticated urban centres grew up along the south coast and they developed a form of writing to deal with the new administration required. The earliest example comes from *Engomi* — unfortunately no-one has yet been able to decipher the script and claims that it resembles the Cretan Linear A script have not helped to uncover its meaning. There does, however, seem to have been strong contact with Greece with a large number of Mycenean settlers arriving at this period. Around 1,400 BC the peace seems to have been further broken by sea-borne raids which devastated many of the coastal towns.

About 300 years later the Phoenecians also began to settle on the island and a large number of small City Kingdoms such as *Kourion*, *Salamis*, *Kition* and *Paphos* grew up. In total there were ten City Kingdoms which were successful in retaining their independence and prosperity despite the attentions of a variety of invading powers. Religion took on a new sophistication and they built temples, mainly to the goddess Astarte, an early manifestation of Aphrodite.

The Assyrians had a brief period of influence when the rulers of the

City Kingdoms submitted to King Sargon II of Assyria and paid him tribute. It seems that the Assyrians left the kings in peace as long as they got their tribute and judging by the riches in the tombs of the kings of *Salamis* they could easily afford this. The kings were the centre of their community around whom a whole cultural life seems to have emerged. There is evidence of epic poetry being written at grand festivals in the temples of Aphrodite at *Kition* and *Palea Paphos*. Some rather partisan commentators claim that Homer was born at *Salamis* and was a participant in these festivals.

With the collapse of the Assyrian Empire the Egyptians took more of an interest in Cyprus. They too were then displaced by the Persians. In the early years, the Cypriot kings retained a good deal of autonomy but as the Persians became more expansionist their rule became more ruthless and there were several revolts against them, inspired by those on the Greek mainland. It was during one of these uprisings that the Persians built the sophisticated siege works still visible on the *Palea Paphos* site.

The most important Cypriot king was Evelthon of *Salamis*. His grandson Onesilos was behind an uprising against the Persians which failed after a great battle at *Amathus* in which Onesilos was killed. The kings were then pacified and joined in the Persian invasion of Athens, much to the confusion of the Athenians. The Greeks still felt they had a claim on Cyprus and in 478BC and 454BC sent fleets to liberate the island. Both times they failed although in the latter case they came close and it was only the death of their General Kimon at *Kition* that meant they had to give up. Kimon became a Cypriot hero and his statue can be seen on the seafront at Larnaca.

The defeat allowed the Persians to strengthen their position until a revolt by Evagoras, the king of *Salamis*, who had a grand plan to unite all the Cypriot kings and bring in the Athenians to fight the Persians. *Kition*, *Soli* and *Amathus* refused to get involved and even after much conspiracy and brute force his plans failed.

Alexander the Great then defeated the Persians and the Cypriot kings were freed. The island was left largely to direct its own affairs and its economy flourished. On Alexander's death Cyprus was subject to dispute between Antigonus and Ptolemy with Ptolemy finally winning control. The island was extremely important to Egypt not least for its copper and wood for building its ships.

250 years later in 58BC the island was annexed by Rome and saw a period of renewed prosperity. Many new buildings were constructed ranging from the theatre of *Soli* to the baths at *Salamis*, reflecting the life of luxury led by the Roman occupiers, if not the local population, and the mosaics in the House of Dionysos at

Paphos reflecting their high artistic standards.

During Roman rule in 45AD St Paul came to Cyprus and converted the Roman Consul to Christianity. In 330AD the Roman Empire split and Cyprus became part of the Byzantine Empire. This was a time of some prosperity marred by the numerous Arab pirate raids which ransacked the coastal cities at frequent intervals. The roads were improved and new industries such as silk production grew up. But it was perhaps the new religion which was the most important driving force in Cyprus at this period, with enormous energy being put into the painting of churches. Many of these depict the entire New Testament and a large number of the paintings are still very well preserved in the churches of the Troodos mountains.

Then the Arab adventurism intensified and their raids led to more permanent occupation as the island swung back from Arab to Byzantine control, reflecting the wider turbulence of the region. Only by 900AD did anything like peace return as the Byzantine empire took permanent control again and a series of governors presided over relative prosperity.

In 1184AD Isaac Comnenos came to the island and proclaimed himself emperor and set up a tyrannical regime. Then in 1191, when the third crusade was under way, Richard I was shipwrecked off Limassol and Comnenos, who had promised Saladin to obstruct the crusaders, was true to his word and harassed Berengaria, Richard's fiancée. As a result Richard attacked Comnenos at Kolossi and then pursued him across the island, engagaing him in a series of battles, right up to the castles of the Karpas where he was captured. Having despatched the enemy, Richard married Berengaria in Limassol castle. Richard then set off for Acre and, needing more money to finance the crusade, sold the island to the Knights Templar. After a few years they found it was too much of a financial burden and the island was given to Guy de Lusignan, a fellow crusader.

The Lusignan period was one of great prosperity, although there was some conflict between the Catholic and Orthodox churches. They ruled the island under a feudal system, encouraged art and culture, built cathedrals in grand Gothic style and extended the castles. Peter I was one of the most spectacular of the Lusignan kings, who travelled the world on crusades and other missions. On his return he had trouble with his wife and mistress and was later found in bed with his head hacked off. His reign was followed by disputes between many members of the family and between Genoese and Venetian merchants. The Genoese managed to get several footholds on the island and between 1374 and 1464 ruled Famagusta. This was part of a rather disastrous period for the island as it suffered with

Chronology of Cyprus

Dates	Period	Sites
7000-3800BC	Neolithic	Choirokoitia
3800-1050BC	Bronze Age	Engomi
1050-50BC	Iron Age	
1050-707BC	Phoenecians	10 City Kingdoms
709-633BC	Assyrians	(Salamis, Kition,
569-525BC	Egyptians	Amathus,Kourion,
525-332BC	Persians	Paphos,Lapithos,
332-323BC	Alexander the Great	Marion, Idalion,
294-50BC	Ptolemies	Tamassos, Soli)
50BC-330AD	Roman	Salamis, Kourion
45AD	visit of St Paul	
330-1191	Split in Roman Empire Byzantine era 7th, 10th century Arab raids	hill churches
1191	Richard I arrival	
1192-1489	Lusignan	Kolossi
1489-1571	Venetian	city walls (Nicosia)
1571-1878	Turkish	mosques
1878-1960	British Rule	
1960	Independence	
1974	Turkish invasion	

plague, earthquakes and drought.

The Venetians annexed the island in 1489 after the marriage of James II to the Venetian Katherine Cornaro and various alleged acts of skulduggery. They neglected Cyprus and it seems to have been a time of decay and poverty. They did, however, devote considerable energy to building up the defences of the cities. Not that it did much good when the Ottoman Turks attacked in 1570. Nicosia fell within days, while Famagusta fell after ten months of bloody fighting.

Unusually the Turks let the Greek Orthodox church survive and the Archbishops retained considerable political power. There were several revolts throughout the seventeenth and eighteenth centuries and then, in 1821 with the outbreak of the War of Independence in Greece, the Turks grew suspicious of the Cypriot church and its leader, Archbishop Kyprianos and many of his bishops were hanged and persecution became widespread.

Towards the end of the century the Turks became concerned about the Russian threat to their northern borders and Cyprus became a burden on their resources, so it was given to the British to administer in 1878. When Turkey took Germany's side in World War I Britain formally annexed the island and brought considerable improvements to the administration and infrastructure of the island.

In the years after the World War II demands for union with Greece (*Enosis*) grew and the local population organised their own plebiscites . By 1955 a terrorist group, EOKA, led by General Grivas, was set up to fight the British, with the aim of achieving union with Greece, and there were many ruthless attacks. During 1954-9, 142 Britons were killed and 492 Greeks. Negotiations opened in 1956 but failed, and Archbishop Makarios, leader of the Cypriot side was deported to the Seychelles.

In 1959 another round of talks were held in London and these led to an agreement which assured independence while giving the British sovereignty over the British bases, a total of 99 square miles. The agreement was implemented in 1960.

Under the agreement there were complicated constitutional arrangements for representation of the Turkish minority, including provision for a Greek president and Turkish vice-president who had a veto on foreign affairs, defence and internal security matters. The police and civil service were to be split 70 per cent to 30 per cent. The agreements proved unworkable and fighting broke out between the Greek and Turkish communities in Nicosia in 1963 and 1964. A UN peace keeping force was sent in to form a buffer between the two communities and the Turks retreated into enclaves.

EOKA (now EOKA B) were still calling for *Enosis* and they masterminded the miltary coup of 1974. Makarios fled and was replaced by Nicos Sampson, an extremist EOKA man. Five days later, on 20 July the Turks invaded, landing at Kyrenia and heavy fighting ensued, culminating in the Turks taking control of 40 per cent of the island. This is now marked by the green line which is patrolled by the United Nations. Subsequent peace talks have all failed and in 1983 the Turkish Cypriots declared themselves an independent state, although this status is only recognised by Turkey.

Despite this division and the problems of rehousing large numbers of refugees the island seems to be prospering. The death of Archbishop Makarios in 1977 did not cause any political problems and the island has a political stability, despite its division, which is rare in the Middle East.

1

EASTERN CYPRUS

This region is a strongly agricultural one, well known for it potato crops which are grown in its distinctive red soil. This intensive use of the land has given rise to a man-made phenomenon on the landscape: a profusion of steel windmills which serve as irrigation pumps, without which the area would be barren and which serve as a clear reminder that water in Cyprus is a precious resource.

The far east of the island has some of the best beaches and since the occupation of the north, has become the subject of extensive holiday development. The traditional tourist centre of Famagusta — which can be seen from the villages of the far east as a now-abandoned ghost town — has been replaced by the ever-expanding resorts on the south coast around Ayia Napa and Protaras.

Leaving Larnaca, the road runs close to the shore although the sea is rarely visible, due first to the oil refinery and then the extensive ribbon development of hotels stretching way out beyond the city on a very busy road. Just off the road, a little inland, is **Livhadia**, a small village known for its basket weaving.

Six miles (10km east) of Larnaca, at the traffic lights, is a public beach run by the tourist organisation, with changing rooms and water sports. This is one of several reasonable beaches in the area.

A couple of miles beyond the crossroads is a turning to **Pyla**, a unique village in that it has a mixed community of Greeks and Turks supervised by the United Nations. It is often held up as an example of how Greeks and Turks can live together in harmony, but there is still a feeling of tension underlined by the military and there is little mixing between the communties. The village is only accessible to residents but it has constructed a kind of annexe on the coast just west of the campsite where there are several good fish restaurants.

Continuing on the main coast road and then turning right one

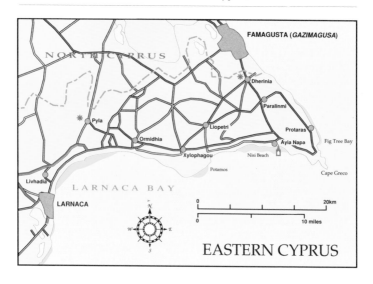

EASTERN CYPRUS

enters the British Sovereign Base of **Dhekalia**. Sovereignty over the bases at Dhekalia, Akrotiri and Episkopi was granted to the British under the Independence settlement and remain of central strategic importance to the British military and indeed NATO.

The whole base contrasts sharply with the surrounding area, the houses are distinctively British and the flashes of green playing fields are unique in summer when everywhere else the grass turns to brown in the heat. Visitors can usually pass through the base easily, although there is a checkpoint at the entrance and occasionally there is a military alert and diversions. The internal roads of the base itself are now sealed off with barbed wire reflecting the increased tensions of recent years. There is an accessible beach just below the CESSAC bookshop which is well stocked with English books.

Beyond Dhekalia, the road continues close to the sea for several

---

British Sovereign Bases

The Sovereign Bases at Dhekalia, Akrotiri and Episkopi were established under the Independence agreement. They cover an area of 99 square miles (257km^2), 2.5 per cent of the land area of Cyprus along with eleven further areas outside the bases on which military training is allowed. The bases are officially British territory and are of considerable strategic importance in the Middle East.

miles passing a few good beaches including those named Romatzos and Paradise which each have their own tavernas on rocky jetties. Visitors can then turn inland to **Ormidhia** which, like many of the villages in this region, has a large refugee population. It dates from the Byzantine period and later was a popular summer resort for the foreign residents of Larnaca. Its church, Ayios Konstantinos Alamos, is said to contain its saint's bones which were found nearby.

There once were numerous archaeological sites in the area but these were destroyed by Cesnola, the American consul in Larnaça in 1865, who was given *carte blanche* to excavate the island's archaeological sites. He uncovered twelve temples and nearly 61,000 tombs. The vast majority of the finds were shipped back to New York and the sites rendered useless for future excavation.

Xylophagou, the next village on the road has a fifteenth-century church dedicated to St George. Its paintings are in a poor state of repair, blackened by smoke from a fire but they are slowly being restored. Those which have been already restored at the eastern end of the church show the Birth of Christ and associated scenes. In the apse is an impressive coat of arms with a double headed eagle, probably the coat of arms of the benefactor of the church. There is also

Fishing boats returning with their catch to Potamos creek

an iconostasis of St George from 1772 and a huge depiction of the Archangel Michael on the north wall.

Off the main road, signed **Potamos**, is a small fishing harbour on a creek. It is an idyllic place, especially early in the morning when the fishermen are returning with their night's catch. The banks of the creek provide a very pleasant place to stroll. At the far end of the track is a rocky but pleasant beach and small church with another walk possible by heading east along the shore. North of the creek is **Liopetri**, a potato growing and basket weaving centre which has an interesting church with an octagonal dome.

Ayia Napa, the next village on this route, was once a quiet remote place; its name meaning wooded glen. These days it is one of the island's busiest tourist centres with discos, restaurants and all the tourist paraphernalia. It is connected by a regular bus service to Larnaca and Paralimni.

A new road leads along the coast passing Makronisos Beach, Golden Beach and Nissi Beach; all of these are extremely pleasant with fine white sand. However, the growth of the resort means that they may now be too crowded and commercialised for the tastes of some. The beaches are linked by a paved walkway.

Nissi beach is still worth a visit, although try and avoid weekends at the height of summer. This was one of the first in the region to be developed and is distinguished by its rocky island just offshore, to which it is possible to wade, crossing on a sand bar. Those who choose to do so should be aware that any exploration of the island may be curtailed for those without shoes as it is made up of extremely sharp rocks.

The Nissi Beach Hotel stands at the eastern end of the beach and there are plenty of water sports facilities and cafés. The next extensive beach is ⅔ mile (1km) away east of Ayia Napa harbour. The harbour is a pleasant enough place with a restaurant at one side, and boat trips around the coast leave from here. The beach itself can be crowded by the residents of the hotels above it.

At its far eastern end, on the headland below the Grecian Bay hotel, are some of the most beautiful sights of this coast. These are spectacular white cliff formations with caves standing out impressively against the distinctive turquoise of the Mediterranean. They are visible from the path in the garden of the hotel or visitors can hire a canoe and explore them by sea. Either way they are definitely worth a detour.

Ayia Napa village contains an enormous number of cafés, restaurants and tourist shops. However, its centre retains some of its old charm mainly due to the presence of the monastery which is a

Easter in Ayia Napa

Easter is one of the most significant festivals in the Greek Ortho-dox church. On the evening of Good Friday there is a grand procession through the village. On Saturday there are church services and outside the church a large bonfire is lit to burn the image of Judas, accompanied by noisy celebration and fireworks. On Easter Sunday there is traditional dancing and singing in the square in front of the monastery.

verdant and peaceful contrast to the bustle of the resort.

The monastery is built over a cave in which an icon of the Virgin was found, allegedly by a hunter chasing his errant dog. It then became a well known shrine visited by pilgrims. The monastery itself was probably founded by a Venetian nobleman's daughter who came here looking for a secluded retreat after her father had refused to let her marry a commoner. She built two churches one Catholic, one Orthodox, which are now under the same roof. The fountain house in the middle of the courtyard was built as her tomb and bears pictures of her father, her mother, herself and a lion chasing a deer.

The church survived the Ottoman Turkish invasion unscathed and was still in use during that period. In 1668 it changed from a women's convent to a monastery and became one of the richest in the region, owning land throughout the area. However, for some un-known reason it was abandoned in the late eighteenth century and fell into disrepair. It was restored in 1813 and again in 1950. The monastery now belongs to the World Council of Churches and serves as a conference centre with the addition of a block of new rooms in which visitors can sometimes stay.

By the south wall is a gateway with a pool overlooked by a huge and ancient sycamore fig tree, where in the evening the cicadas gather and sing in one of the most distinctive sounds of Cyprus. Below here a huge new church has been built.

Outside the monastery is the centre of the village and the main square where there are theatrical performances during the Ayia Napa festival. In the evenings it is a lively place, with impromptu portrait painters and stalls selling souvenirs, all of which which can be observed from the bars round the side of the square. The post office is up the hill to the northeast of the monastery and the tourist office is downhill on the road leading to the harbour.

Ayia Napa's one-way system is confusing and visitors wanting to head further east should take the road, signed first to Paralimni and then to Cape Greco. Cape Greco is 2 miles (3km) off the main route on a narrow but newly tarred road. There is also a bumpy dirt track to the high point of the cape. The cape has not been developed because there is a miltary listening post on the far headland. The coast is very rocky but the outlook is very beautiful and it is possible to clamber down to the sea.

The main road itself offers spectacular views of the sea below. It then reaches **Protaras**, a resort which has grown in the past ten years from nothing to be a major tourist centre. It now has shops, banks, hotels and restuarants but no real focus and out of season it must be a sad sort of place. It caters for all the excesses of the undiscerning holidaymaker and should be avoided by all those to whom discos do not appeal.

Fig Tree Bay beach was much of the reason for the development of Protaras, in fact it used to be the only attraction of this part of the island. The beach is marked by a fig tree which, according to a sign at the café, was brought by invaders in the seventeenth century. The beach is sandy and well known for it water sports facilities especially its water skiing. It also has an offshore island to which the energetic can swim and gain a little seclusion because the main beach can be very crowded, especially at weekends.

There are numerous coves, accessible from the main road beyond Protaras. The best is perhaps that just outside Paralimni at the sign for Ayios Trias. This is a pleasant little bay which is quieter than the beaches further south. It has a restaurant on one side and a small church on the headland at the other.

Paralimni is a long straggly village with a maze of streets with a resident population of 6,000. It used to be a small farming community but now its main occupation is clearly tourism, although it is several miles from the sea. There are three churches in the centre. The most interesting, on the roundabout, was built in the thirteenth century and has some interesting eighteenth-century plates. The other two churches are large and modern.

The village has a certain notoriety amongst bird lovers as the centre of the hunting of the *ambelopoulia* or black cap. This poor creature is lured onto sticks coated with lime from which it cannot escape and is then eaten as a delicacy, apparently best crunched whole, having first removed a poisonous part.

From Paralimni one can drive to **Dherinia**, the nearest village to Famagusta. Famagusta is part of the area occupied by the Turks and has been left empty since the 1974 invasion. There is one enterprising villager who has set himself up as an 'official' information centre and

The fountain at Ayia Napa monastery

Cliffs and hotel development at Grecian Bay

viewing point, inviting visitors onto his rooftop where there is a telescope to allow the inquisitive tourist to get a better view of the ghost town and the checkpoint.

Dherinia also has three churches, Ayios Georghios, Ayia Marina and Panayia which has fine seventeenth-century icons. The route then turns back to Sotira and Liopetri. These are typical Cypriot farming villages, each with their ubiquitous churches, coffee shops and occasional supermarket. The road then rejoins the earlier route to Xylophagou and back to Larnaca.

Additional Information

Accommodation
There is an abundance of hotels in the area. However, the vast majority are prebooked by those on package deals and at the height of the season independent visitors should not rely on finding a room.

Campsites
Ayia Napa
Opposite Nisi Beach
Open: March-October

Boating
Boat trips from Ayia Napa harbour to Paralimni and Protoras and to the 'forbidden city' of Famagusta, although the boats can only remain offshore at a distance.

Places to Visit
Ayia Napa Monastery
Buildings open all day, church is usually kept locked.

Local Events
Easter
Very important celebration in Ayia Napa culminating in a bonfire at midnight on Easter Saturday.

Festival of Cataclysmos
Held at Penetcost. Involves three days of festivities on the beach ranging from dancing and singing to boat races.

September
Ayia Napa festival with music and folk art exhibitions.

In the summer there are displays of folk dancing and traditional music in Ayia Napa square every Sunday.

Sports Facilities
Sea sports and fishing
All along the coast.

Tennis
Courts are available at many of the larger hotels.

Riding
Cape Greco Equestrian Centre
Near Cape Greco

Tourist Offices
17 Archbishop Makarios Avenue
Ayia Napa
☎ 03 721796

Transport
From Ayia Napa to Larnaca and Nicosia: EMAN Bus. Bus station is on road to the harbour
There are also buses from Ayia Napa to Paralimni.

Emergencies
Paralimni Hospital
☎ 06 232364
Police stations in Ayia Napa
(☎ 21553) and Paralimni (☎ 21417)

2

LARNACA

Situated on the south coast **Larnaca** (Larnaka), with its international airport to the southwest, is the point of entry to the island
for many visitors. The airport was built after the Turkish invasion of
1974 when Nicosia airport was put under UN control. Its construction led to the development of this, once quiet, town into the major
tourist centre that it is today.

The present city is built on the ancient site of *Kition*. According to
legend it was founded by by Kitim, one of Noah's grandsons. It was
then inhabited by the Myceneans but was destroyed in 1,200BC,
along with other coastal towns, possibly by seaborne invaders.
Reconstruction followed, but an earthquake in around 1,075BC
devastated the city again.

A new city was built by the Achaeans and the Phoenecians in the
ruins and by the ninth century BC it had become an important
trading centre, with its main export being copper from the mines at
Tamassus. It was extensively damaged in the wars with the Persians
and in 450BC was besieged by the Greek fleet, led by General Kimon
with 200 triremes. Both the leading generals were killed in the
ensuing battle and the Athenians gave up the struggle, leaving the
town in the hands of pro-Persian forces.

Larnaca's most famous son was Zeno, the ancient Greek philoso-
pher. He was born here in 335BC and then went to Athens in 312BC
where he lectured at Stoa Poikile (painted colonnade) which is
thought to have been the source of the name of the Stoic movement.
Zeno taught that happiness came from conforming to divine reason,
accepting cheerfully whatever happened. He died in Athens in
263BC. A bust commemorating him can be seen at the junction of
Nikodimou Mylona Street and Grigori Afxentiou Avenue.

After a further turbulent period of history, the town was destroyed

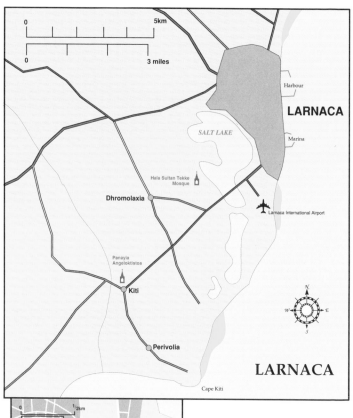

Monument to Kimon the Athenian on the seafront at Larnaca

Ayios Lazaros, Larnaca

in a fire in 250BC. As a result it was of little significance during the Roman and Byzantine periods. However, when the Genoese attacked Famagusta many traders fled to Larnaca and the town began to grow again. This continued into the Turkish period when it became a major centre for foreign traders and the base for many of the foreign consulates. Among others, the British Levant company operated out of Larnaca, exporting silk back to England. When the British took over control of the island they moved the administration to Nicosia and the town went into decline again until its renaissance as a tourist and industrial centre today.

The tourist areas can be divided into three sections: the centre of town, the small resorts beyond the airport, and the extensive development out on the Dhekalia road. Visitors staying in these last two areas will need some form of transport to get into town, although many of the hotels have their own facilities and mini-resorts have grown up around them to cater for the tourists. While there is an abundance of apartment blocks in the town centre, the independent traveller will have difficulty in finding accommodation, especially at the height of the season. There are plenty of restaurants particularly along the seafront, although it has to be said that many of these establishments are aimed at the less discerning tourist.

The town can get very busy, with its one-way system adding to the confusion. If possible drivers should avoid the narrow streets behind the seafront, especially at rush hour. Parking, too, can be difficult, there is a car park by the marina and another at the opposite end of the seafront near the mosque.

The seafront is perhaps the best place to start any exploration of the town. At the far western end of the promenade is the **Turkish fort**. This dates from 1625 and was built by the Turks to defend the city but was more often used as a prison, especially when the island was under British control. It is now a museum and has exhibits from the site of *Kition*. In summer there are occasional performances of folk dancing in its courtyard. Climbing up on the walls offers good views out to sea. The fort is literally on the seashore and visitors can walk around the sea wall with the water lapping at their feet. Beyond the fort, to the west, stretches a long road of shops and cafés behind a narrow gravelly beach.

Next to the fort is the mosque of **Djami Kebir** built in the sixteenth century, now known as the grand mosque of Larnaca, which is still used by Muslims in the city. Close by is another mosque, built when this was the Turkish area of Larnaca and a part of the building is now the youth hostel.

The promenade which runs along the seafront, parallel to Zinonos

Kitieos, is lined with palm trees, cafés and English-style pubs. Surprisingly the beach is very popular, despite it being man-made and one of the least impressive on the island.

Halfway along the seafront is the statue of the Classical Greek naval officer Kimon who died here in a great battle with the Persians. He came with a fleet of 200 triremes but was defeated by the Persian forces. The inscription reads, ' Though dead he was victorious', and today people with problems are advised to consult the statue in the hope that it will offer solutions to their difficulties.

There is a large marina with berths for several hundred yachts. The marina is closed to the public but visitors may like to stroll along the adjacent jetty or swim from the breakwater. Just inland from the marina, in a small shady garden, is the tourist office. Turning left beyond the tourist office is Zinonos Kitieos street, the main shopping area with carpets, sheepskin rugs and brasswork much in evidence, along with the more usual tourist souvenirs.

About halfway along the street is the **Pierides Museum** of Cypriot antiquities, which was founded in 1839. It is located in a pleasant, grey shuttered eighteenth-century house and the exhibits are from the private collection of Demetrios Pierides, a Cypriot scholar and archaeologist, and were later added to by other members of his family. It has 2,500 exhibits which range from the Neolithic to the medieval periods.

The collection is in four rooms. The first contains Neolithic pottery and various representations of goddesses, along with bowls used in rituals which are decorated with depictions of birds. Room 2 contains more pottery with pictures of birds and fishes and figurines used in religious rites. Room 3 includes jugs from the site at *Marion*, alabaster vases and a mask on the wall. Room 4 has pottery from the medieval period and a collection of glass along with some jewellery. In the hall is an inscription from a grave found in *Kition* and three shields depicting lions and a sculpture of a flamingo. There are some early maps of Cyprus on the walls.

The road from the museum leads to the main shopping streets of the town and the market. The market is a good place to buy copper and silver items. Opposite the market is **Ayios Lazaros** church. This was built in the ninth century by Emperor Leo VI. Its white painted belfry is highly distinctive and escaped the Turkish ban on such structures, who feared that the Christians would use them for military purposes. The church is in the centre of a square surrounded by cloisters.

It has four domes over the nave and the roof is supported on four sets of double columns. The pulpit is of ingenious construction, being placed in one of these columns and is lavishly decorated in gilt. In another there is a silver icon from 1659, with a picture of Lazaros himself. There are also good paintings of the Virgin and Child and St George and the Dragon. The iconostasis or screen between the altar and the main church is a good example of wood carving in baroque style. The saint's empty tomb is down some steps under the sanctuary. Eight days before Easter the icon of Lazaros is carried in a procession led by the Bishop of Kition to the marina. On the doors are Byzantine and Lusignan coats of arms.

Just behind the church is the English cemetery which contains the graves of various British consuls and members of the British Levant company as well as those of visiting seamen.

A good walk up the road, heading away from the seafront, is the church of **Ayia Phaneromeni** built next to two tombs cut out of the rock which could date from 80BC. The church is supposed to have mystical powers to cure illnesses if the afflicted walk round it three times and leave behind a piece of their clothing. At the far end of this

The Muslim shrine of Hala Sultan Tekke, by the Salt Lake, Larnaca

road are the Public Gardens which are typical dusty places, although they offer the chance to get away from the bustle of the traffic.

In eastern Larnaca is the archaeological site of *Kition*. It is reached by turning inland, along Kimonos and the site is spread around Kilkis Avenue and onto Leontiou Machaira Street. Lying in the suburbs of Larnaca, it is only sporadically signposted and not easy to find.

Kition was an important City Kingdom and its remains go as far back as 1,300BC. Initially, it was surrounded by a mud wall with two bastions at the northern end of the city, which are still visible. There was some sort of catastrophe between 1,075 and 1,050BC when the walls collapsed, but *Kition* was later rebuilt and became a flourishing Phoenecian settlement.

The modern city covers most of the site but there are several parts worth visiting. The first is the Mycenean site, on Kimonos, first excavated in 1962-3 and where a large amount of pottery, ornaments and jewellery were found.

The main site is on Leontiou Machaira street. Excavations are still

Icons in the church of Panayia Angeloktistos, Kiti

going on and visitors can observe these from a raised wooden platform. The earliest discoveries were from the thirteenth century BC with a Mycenean city built on top. The main points to look for are the remains of the city wall made from gigantic blocks of stone and a temple which was rebuilt several times to different deities, the last by the Phoenecians to Astarte. Some outlines of ships can be seen on the wall. Visitors can see other sites in the area although they may be restricted by the ongoing excavation.

Nearby, on the junction of Kimonos and Kilkis streets in Kalogreon square, is the **District Museum**. The first room displays sculpture, mainly female torsos and terracotta figurines. The next room houses the pottery collection from *Kition* and Livhadia, a village just east of Larnaca, with Mycenean vases and a variety of ornaments in bronze, clay and glass. There are also some Neolithic artefacts from *Chorokoitia* and some glass from the Roman era. In the garden are numerous torsos of statues.

Uphill, north of the museum used to be the *Acropolis* which was built in thirteenth century BC. However, it was levelled by the British army to fill in marshland to destroy the habitat of the malaria mosquito, with the result that nothing much is visible to the visitor, although malaria has indeed been eliminated from the island.

The town's beaches are not very impressive, with one man-made stretch of dark sand. There are extensive beaches east of the town where most of the hotels have been built. To the west too, there are a few reasonable beaches, the best being around the Cape Kiti area.

Just outside Larnaca is the newly built open-air municipal amphitheatre, which holds various theatrical performances as part of the Larnaca Festival. The tourist office has details.

Excursions out of Larnaca

Just east of the town, off the airport road, is Makenzie beach which is popular with the locals and has long supported a large number of makeshift cafés along its dark shingle. It is not a peaceful place being so close to the airport and can be busy, especially at weekends.

The **Salt Lake**, just off the airport road, is one of the most distinctive landmarks of the area, having an area of 1.2 square miles (3.2km^2). In winter it fills with water and attracts large numbers of migrating birds, including flamingoes which form a blaze of pink as they gather in the centre of the lake. In summer the water evaporates leaving a crust of salt and a haze of grey dust.

According to legend the lake's saltiness stems from St Lazaros' request of an old woman for food and drink. She refused, saying her vines had dried up, to which he said 'may your vines be dry and be a salt lake forever more'. A more likely explanation is that the salt water penetrates the porous rock between the lake and the sea, making the water salty. The salt used to be one of the island's major exports being collected by donkeys and carried to the edge of the lake to form huge pyramids. These days only 3,500 tons are collected each year.

Dominating the lake, on its western shore, is the Hala Sultan Tekke. It is a famous Muslim shrine standing amidst the palm trees. It contains the tomb of Umm Haram who, according to legend, was an aunt or even godmother of the prophet of Mohammed. She came to Larnaca in 647, but fell from her mule and broke her neck and was buried here. The Turks built the mosque in 1816 and her tomb is inside the mosque beneath two huge stones 18ft (5.5m) high. The Tekke is signposted from the airport road. Visitors can enter if they are suitably dressed and if they remove their shoes.

There is also a Bronze Age settlement in the vicinity dating from 1600BC. Excavations have taken place since 1897 and some of the best finds are in the British Museum and show the influence of the Minoans and the Pharaohs on Cyprus during that period. It seems that the site was a copper trading centre with extensive links to other communities around the Mediterranean. There is another such site at the nearby village of **Dhromolaxia** (1½ miles, 2km, west of the Tekke) but there is little for the amateur to see.

Kiti is the next place of interest close to Larnaca. It is famous for the church of Panayia Angeloktistos. The name means 'built by angels' and it dates from the fifth century although it has been rebuilt many times since. There are many fine icons and mosaics and outside is a pleasant garden.

The finest mosaic depicts the Virgin Mary with Jesus with the Archangels Gabriel and Michael on either side and is of exceptional quality. She is standing on a footstool with Christ in her left arm. It is an extremely delicate design and much more naturalistic in style than other contemporary paintings. This has puzzled many Byzantine scholars and they have been unable to determine exactly when it was painted, although now there is a consensus that it belongs to the sixth century. The mosaic will be lit up if visitors ask. A small chapel attached to the north end of the church has some good fifteenth-century paintings, including one of St George. In the village is a bridge which was once part of a medieval castle destroyed by the Arabs.

Cape Kiti is becoming a tourist centre and both Kiti and the next village **Perivolia** have several shops, banks and cafés and development is taking place all along the road to the coast. There is a modern

❋
❋ lighthouse, by a modern one and the ruins of a Phoenecian temple. A further site of interest is a Venetian watchtower. Visitors cannot enter the tower but can see the coat of arms of the lion of St Mark. There is a shipwreck from the Byzantine period lying offshore. The beach is pleasant enough, being a long stretch of shingle which is popular with local residents.

❋ On the road west out of Larnaca, particularly noticeable to those coming into the town from Limassol, is the Kamares aqueduct. It was built in 1746 by the Turks to provide water for the town. It consists of thirty-three arches which are still in good condition today, although it ceased to be used as an aqueduct in 1939.

Additional Information

Accommodation
Camping
Forest Beach Camping
☎ 04 622414
5 miles (8km) east of Larnaca town centre.
78 places
Open: April-October

Youth Hostel
27 Nicolaou Rossou St
(near St Lazaros Church)
Larnaca
☎ c/o 04 621580
Open all year round

Boat Trips
From Larnaca harbour along the coast to Ayia Napa.

Marina
☎ 04 653110
There is an extensive marina at Larnaca with berths for up to 400 boats with good facilities. It is ten minutes walk from the town centre.

Fishing
Lefkara Dam
Near Lefkara village, 25 miles (40km) north of Larnaca

Lymbia Dam
13 miles (21km) northwest of Larnaca town

Kalavassos Dam
Nicosia-Limasol road

Larnaca
Fishing shelter east of Larnaca airport, has boats available for sea fishing.

District Fisheries Department
Piale Pasha Avenue
Larnaca
☎ 04 630294

Local Events
Epiphany
In common with other coastal towns, Epiphany is celebrated in Larnaca by the throwing of a cross into the sea.

March 30
The procession of the icon of St Lazaros
A special service is held in memory of the saint followed by a procession along the promenade.

Cataclysmos
Last week in May

Larnaca Festival
July 1-31
The festival takes place in the courtyard of the fort and includes dance, theatre, music and exhibitions of paintings.

Places to Visit

Kition Archaeological Site
Open: May-Sept Mon-Sat 7.30am-1.30pm; Oct-Apr Mon-Fri 7.30am-2pm, Sat 7.30am-1pm

Larnaca District Archaeological Museum
☎ 04 630169
Open: May-Sept Mon-Sat 7.30am-1.30pm; Oct-Apr Mon-Fri 7.30am-2pm, Sat 7.30am-1.30pm

The Pierides Museum
Open: all year round Mon-Sat 9am-1pm

Larnaca Fort
Open: May-Sept Mon-Sat 7.30am-7.30pm; Oct-Apr 7.30am-sunset

Hala Sultan Tekke
Open: May-Sept daily 7.30am-7.30pm; Oct-Apr daily 7.30am to sunset

Sport

There are two athletics stadia in the Larnaca area, including Zeno stadium on Artemides Avenue which also has a swimming pool.

Shooting
Larnaca shooting club
Kamares (3 miles, 4km, from the city centre)
Skeet and trap facilities
Open: Wednesday, Saturday and Sunday

Swimming:
Larnaca public beach 6 miles (10km) east of town

Tennis
Larnaca tennis Club
Kilkis Street
☎ 04 656999

Tourist Offices

Larnaca Airport
☎ 04 654389
Open 24 hours

Democratias Square
(by the marina)
Larnaca
☎ 04 654322

Transport

Bus stops for all buses can be found in Hermes Street, Larnaca.
To the airport: bus no 21 from Athens Avenue, opposite the town hall.
To Nicosia: Kallenos Bus Co (☎ 04 654890) from opposite the Sun Hall Hotel
To Limassol: Kallenos Bus Co, Sun Hall Hotel.
To Paphos: via Limassol, no direct services.
To Ayia Napa: EMAN Ayia Napa Bus, from opposite the Sun Hall.
There are numerous services to some of the mountain villages and smaller resort, details from the tourist office.

Entertainment

Open air municipal amphitheatre.
Performances of Greek drama during Larnaca festival.
West side of Artemides Avenue, south of turning to Limassol.

Emergencies

Larnaca General hospital
☎ 04 630311

General emergencies ☎199

3

SOUTH OF NICOSIA

This area of the island, consisting mainly of the Mesaoria plain, can seem barren and dusty, especially in summer. These days many visitors pass through the area rapidly on their way to Limassol or Larnaca on the new dual carriageway.

Across the Island to Larnaca

To reach Larnaca from Nicosia it is necessary first to take the Limassol road and then those who wish to cross the island as quickly as possible should take the new Larnaca road which forks away to the east at Perakhorio, 11 miles (17½ km) from Nicosia, from where it is a very quick journey.

Alternatively one can turn at Nisou to Dhali, taking the old road. There is something of a maze of roads crossing under and around the dual carriageway, but once found the old road passes by **Perakhorio** where there is a church of the Holy Apostles with twelfth-century frescoes. The church, on a hill just southwest of the village, is a small rounded structure with numerous arched recesses. Only a few paintings have survived but these include Christ Pantokrator in the dome, the Annunciation and the depiction of numerous saints. They are dated, on account of their style, to 1160 which makes them some of the earliest paintings on the island.

In **Dhali** is another small sandstone church, built in 1317 with an interesting picture of the donors. Just beyond Dhali is *Idalion*, an ancient Bronze Age site and traces of the settlement, mainly ruins of the city walls, are still visible although nothing very impressive. It was once one of the ten City Kingdoms of the island and a centre of worship of Aphrodite. According to legend Adonis was killed near here by a bear or possibly a boar while he was hunting; a pursuit which Aphrodite had repeatedly tried to persuade him to give up.

One can continue to Lymbia and then take a diversion north to **Athienou** which was an ancient metal centre and now an agricultural village. *Golgoi* nearby, was an ancient settlement, founded, according to legend by Golgos the son of Aphrodite and Adonis. Its archaeology was destroyed by the frantic digging of Cesnola, the American consul who made full use of his permission to excavate the sites of the island. He uncovered some huge sculptured heads which were over 3ft (1m) high and some statues which are 8ft (2½m) tall, which are now in the Metropolitan Museum in New York. The large number of bronze objects found here have suggested to some archaeologists that the people found some religious significance in metallurgy and that *Golgoi* could have been on the route from the copper mines to the harbour.

The landscape is barren and occasionally sinister as the road passes beneath the Turkish lookout posts sited on the hills and the Turkish crescents chalked out of the hill remind the visitor of the island's division.

Returning south the road runs rapidly into Larnaca, perhaps taking a slight diversion to Aradhipou, east of the main road. Aradhipou is a major agricultural centre and was once the site of the residence of Hugh IV in 1352. However, it was burned by the Arabs and only regained any importance when it became part of the camel route from Larnaca to Nicosia.

From Nicosia to Limassol

The 50 miles (80km) to Limassol can be covered rapidly along the new dual carriageway. The first site of interest is beyond the crossroads at Perakhorio and the turn to Larnaca. This is the village of **Alambra**, the site of a Bronze Age settlement where excavations have been taking place since 1974. Some remains have been uncovered but the casual visitor may be a little disappointed by the site.

Off the road (20 miles, 32km from Nicosia) to the east is the village of **Pyrga**, well signed from junction 11 off the main road. It has two churches and a mosque. One of these, at the entrance to the village, is the royal chapel of Ayia Ekaterini, also known as the Chapelle Royale, a Latin chapel built by the Lusignans in 1421. It is a very small building, only about 20 by 12ft (6 x 4m), with a single aisle. Inside there is a painting of its founders King Janus and his wife, Charlotte de Bourbon, who are also present in the painting of the Crucifixion. The usual New Testament cycle of paintings can be seen although only fragments of many of the paintings have survived. The Last Supper is the best preserved while those of the life of the Virgin Mary on the west wall are hard to make out. The Department of Antiquities

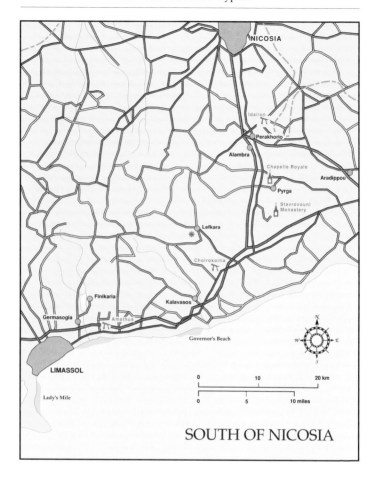

SOUTH OF NICOSIA

is now restoring the paintings, but if the church is locked ask for the key at the coffee shop.

The Church of Ayia Marina is the other church in the village and was probably built in the fourteenth or fifteenth century. It contains many paintings, but they will have to be cleaned before their true value can be assessed.

Back on the main road is the turning to **Stavrovouni** monastery, which lies 6 miles (9½km) up a new road at a height of 2,300ft (698m). The road passes a military camp where photography is banned. Then comes a subordinate monastery, Ayia Varnava, where there is a

Lacemaking

Embroidery, crochet and lace making have been practised in Cyprus for 2,000 years. Evidence has been found at Salamis of embroidery influenced by the Assyrians, and the craft seems to have been passed down since then and still appear to be the main hobby of older Cypriot women.

It was during the Venetian period that Lefkara gained its reputation as a lace-making centre. It was a popular summer resort for Venetian nobles who brought their fine cloths and seamstresses with them.

In 1889 Theofyla Antoni set up a school to teach lace making in Lefkara. She was clearly a woman of some force and made several business trips to Egypt to sell her lace. The lace became known as *lefkaritika* and the village's fame was fully established.

modern icon painter whose skills are widely advertised. There are large signs by the side of the road advising that women are not allowed into Stavrovouni. Women who decide to drive up to the top of the hill may find the impressive views compensate for the sexist attitude of the monks.

The whole mountain has long been important in religious terms. In the Classical period, pilgrims came to a temple to Aphrodite at its summit. In 327 AD the Empress Helena (Constantine's mother) is said to have brought a part of the Holy Cross here and founded the monastery. In 1426 it was burned by the Arabs and again by the Turks in 1570. The monks returned a century later, although the current monastery was built in the nineteenth century.

The buildings themselves are therefore of little historical interest and are now guarded by large wooden gates. Inside, however, is the monastery's main treasure, the fragment of the cross now ornately covered up. The monks may show some visitors the skulls of previous monks, and this is regarded as an immense privilege.

The energetic may want to walk up to the monastery by a relatively short but fairly steep climb. The path starts from Ayia Varnava monastery just past the army camp and passes some beehives. After a sharp bend to the left the path climbs uphill and it should take about 45 minutes to reach the top. Alternatively one can walk up the road and climb directly up its terraces, when feeling energetic, to avoid the long bends.

Continuing on the main Limassol road is a turning right, or west, into the hills up a steep climb for 5½ miles (9km) to **Lefkara**. Situated at a height of 1,950ft (585m) this is a very popular tourist destination with numerous cafés and tourist shops and is served by buses from the major towns. The village consists of two halves, Pano (lower) and Kato (upper).

It had a traumatic history, as it was the site of two major battles, the first was between Richard I and Comnenos in the twelfth century and one in 1426 between Arabs and King Janus. Then it was sacked by the Venetians and many of its inhabitants were massacred.

It is now famous for its lace, called *lefkaritika* and its embroidery. Leonardo da Vinci is reputed to have bought lace here for Milan cathedral in 1481. Nowadays it is possible to see the women of the village still working on this craft although today many are wise to the potential for profit in their work and tourists should beware of buying the first wares they are offered. There is a small museum of lace making and silverware in the restored House of Patsalos. The village is also known for its Loukoumia or Turkish delight which it may be possible to see being made.

Lefkara is characterised by its narrow streets and houses which are built around courtyards with balconies in an Italian style rather than the usual Cypriot mountain village design. While the main street is set up totally for tourists the narrow alleyways off on either side remain unspoilt and extremely pleasant places to wander.

In Kato Lefkara is a single-aisled church with paintings from the twelfth century while the Church of the Holy Cross in Pano Lefkara has beautiful eighteenth-century icons and a silver cross from the thirteenth century. Both churches offer impressive views of the surrounding countryside. There is a religious fair on 13-14 September to celebrate the day of the Holy Cross.

The lower village has a totally different atmosphere to its elevated sister. Its streets are even narrower and more labyrinthine, lined by distinctive blue painted houses. There are some shops here but the 'hard sell' of the upper village is engagingly lacking.

A short distance off the main Nicosia to Limassol dual carriageway (junction 14) is the ancient site of *Choirokoitia* (*Khirokitia*). It is a significant site mainly because it is so old. It was one of the earliest Neolithic settlements dating from 6,800 BC and was first excavated in 1934. Excavations still continue today. As is often the case with such sites the casual visitor may find it hard to make out anything from the piles of stones.

The site is well placed in fertile land with a permanent water supply and occupies a good defensive position on the hill, surrounded by a large wall about 3ft (1m) thick. The main occupation of the residents seems to have been agriculture and many agricultural implements have been found. This area contains the bases of the unique beehive-shape houses. Stones from the river were used for the foundations and then mud bricks were added on top and there were even some multistorey houses.

There seem to have been two sizes of house, those with a diameter of 10-12ft (3-4m) and those about 24-27ft (7-8m). The largest house, called Tholos I, is part of a complex of buildings and must have belonged to the most important family. Each hut had a flattened earth floor, raised platforms at the edges for sleeping, some sort of fireplace and a central pole to support the roof. The houses were built close together and linked by narrow passageways across the hillside.

Clearly it was a very densely populated place. Eight layers of habitation were found in some areas with twenty-six bodies in one house. Graves were dug either in the floor of the house or just outside. The bodies were found in a contracted position with a large stone on their chests, perhaps suggesting a fear of the dead. The large number of children's bodies suggest a very high infant mortality rate.

The site has four areas. One enters through some modern steps to the main street which is still visible today. In this area are significant remains of the beehive-shaped houses and in the middle is a larger house, up to 29ft (9m) in diameter. The second area, further up the road, has houses B and C which contained numerous burials. Area 3 has several mudbrick houses, including house F which contained twenty-six burials. The final area is at the far end of the site up the hill. From here it is possible to get a clearer impression of the site as a whole, which is otherwise quite confusing. This part contains the earliest building.

Many rich finds have been made at *Choirokoitia*. They included decorated bowls and human figures in grey green rock. A clay human head sculpted in a naturalistic way was one of the most interesting artefacts which, along with all the finds from the site, is in the Cyprus Museum in Nicosia.

A couple of miles west of *Choirokoitia* and 1½ miles (2½km) off the main road at **Kalavasos** is another Neolithic settlement. The site is across the river from the modern day village. A number of circular huts with plastered walls were found here. On these walls traces of paintings have been uncovered, including what seems to be a depiction of a human figure. The same sort of burials are found here as at *Choirokoitia*. There are numerous other settlements in the area which probably housed those who worked at the nearby copper mines. Excavations are still in progress at all these sites and they may not always be fully accessible to the public.

The Coast to Limassol

As the road reaches the coast there are plenty of possibilities for confusion for unwary drivers with the old and new roads running almost parallel for much of the way. The new road is obviously faster and allows for less exploration, although it has to be said that the landscape in this area is not especially impressive. In particular the cement works on the headland does not help to improve the view. Visitors might as well take the new road until Amathus where the old road provides a more interesting drive.

There is one good beach in the area. It is signposted **Governor's Beach** from the main road and is a short distance away. There is a large campsite here and a taverna on the clifftop. The beach lies down some steps at the bottom of white cliffs, which stand in sharp contrast to its dark sand which gets uncomfortably hot in summer. The beach is quite small and can get busy at weekends.

From Governor's Beach the road runs fairly close to the shore and soon meets the outskirts of the ever expanding tourist development of Limassol where the hotels block access to the sea. Five miles (8km) outside Limassol is the site of *Amathus* which was a very early settlement and was important right through to Byzantine times when Richard the Lionheart landed here with his fleet in 1191.

The first inhabitants were probably Mycenean although there is no definite evidence to prove this. It was important because of its port from where it exported copper and timber. The golden age of *Amathus* was during the Hellenistic and Roman period, but then it suffered extensive damage in the earthquakes of the fourth century. It was then rebuilt only to be pillaged by the Arabs.

The site is large and stretches eastwards from the Amathus Beach Hotel, where the *Acropolis* and lower town once were, for 2 miles (3km) to where there used to be a *Necropolis*. The most easily visible feature of the site is the *Agora* which is in a fenced area signposted off the road. There are a large number of pillars, some of which have been restored and the vestiges of some of the early walls. On the hill above are the remains of the *Acropolis* and a Temple to Aphrodite with a large stone jar marking its entrance. At the bottom of the hill is an early Christian basilica.

The other main feature of *Amathus* are the tombs. In the *Western Necropolis*, in the grounds of the Amathus Beach Hotel, is an underground tomb. There are other tombs across the road. A little further east is an open area with another tomb which has three chambers. Crossing over the river, usually dried up, the visitor reaches the line of the of city wall which stretches out onto a promontory and juts out into the sea marking the site of an old harbour.

A wide variety of local food is available

The 'White Lands' north of Larnaca

The visitor can turn inland at the Ayia Varnava church, going up the track to the *Eastern Necropolis* where there are more tombs and a water cistern. There have been numerous significant finds here, including a sarcophagus now in the Metropolitan Museum in New York. A limestone jar from the sixth century BC, 6ft (1.85m) high and 6½ft (2.2m) circumference with four huge handles, was found here. It is now in the Louvre in Paris and reputedly it took eight days to get it from the hill to the sea even with the help of fifty sailors. Today excavations are concentrated on the area between the *Acropolis* and the *Eastern Necropolis* where the lower city used to be.

The approach to Limassol is characterised by a long line of hotels stretched on either side of the road. Just outside the town, crammed in between the hotels, is **Dhassoudi** beach which has a wide range of sporting facilities and is run by the tourist organisation. There is also public access to many of the beaches even where hotels have been built.

An interesting excursion is to **Germasogia** (Yermasoyia), just northeast of Limassol. The village was fortified in the medieval period by the Knights Templar. However, its main interest today is its dam which was built in 1968. It is a popular picnic spot and a pleasant change from a day on the beach, although in the height of summer the reservoir may be fairly empty. There are several other villages, such as **Finikaria**, near the dam which have pleasant cafés and good views of the surrounding area.

Additional Information

Accommodation
Camping
Governor's Beach
☎ 05 632300
Space for 247 tents, 111 caravans
Open: April to October

Places to Visit
Choirokoitia Archaeological Site
(Junction 14 off the Limassol-
Nicosia road)
Open: daily except Monday, May-
Sept 7.30am-7.30pm; Oct-Apr
7.30am until sunset

Chappelle Royale
Pyrga
(junction 11 off Limassol-Nicosia
road)
Key from the café in the village

Stavrovouni Monastery
(junction 11 off the Limassol-
Nicosia road)
Open sunrise-sunset, except siesta
between 12 noon and 1pm (3pm
May-Sept)
Women may not enter the monastery.

Transport
Buses to Lefkara from Limassol.

4

LIMASSOL AND THE AKROTIRI PENINSULA

L imassol lies on the south coast and as the island's main port often has a long line of cargo ships lying offshore. Those arriving in Cyprus by sea will disembark at Limassol. The town offers easy access to the rest of the island, being linked to Nicosia on a fast new dual carriageway, while the Troodos mountains lie a short drive to the north.

Limassol, with a population of just over 120,000, is the main commercial and industrial centre of the island and can therefore be a little disappointing for the visitor. Nonetheless, it is increasingly being marketed as a holiday destination with a large number of hotels strung out along the roads leading out of the city. This is especially true of the old Nicosia road which is lined with hotels in a seemingly everlasting strip of development.

The city itself has little ancient history; although tombs have been found in the surrounding area, *Amathus* and *Kourion* were clearly much more important sites. Limassol seems to have come to prominence only in the medieval period when Richard the Lionheart, travelling to the crusades, was shipwrecked here. King Richard of England, more well known for his exploits in France and for his connection with King John and Robin Hood, organised the Third Crusade to try and regain Jerusalem from Saladin. He sailed with his fleet and his fiancée, Berengaria, bound for Syria but was caught in a storm and ended up in Limassol. The then ruler of the island, Isaac Comnenos, had promised not to allow any crusader's ships into his ports. True to his word he made life difficult for Richard, harassing Berengaria who had been forced ashore after her ship was wrecked. After these various nefarious acts against Richard's ships, a full battle broke out near Kolossi. Comnenos was beaten and retreated back across the island and onto the Karpas peninsula where he was

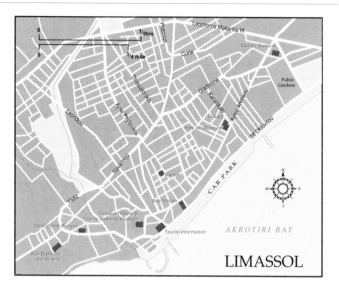

LIMASSOL

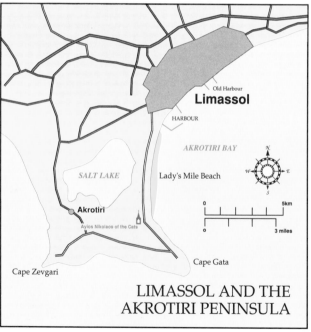

LIMASSOL AND THE
AKROTIRI PENINSULA

finally captured. Richard then married Berengaria and carried on to Acre.

The whole adventure turned out well for Richard as he sold the island to the Knights Templar for a significant sum but they found a few years later that that they could not afford to run it, so the island was passed back to Richard who then gave it to Guy de Lusignan, but kept the money initially paid for it. The island then became a base for the Crusaders, with various European monarchs pausing here on their way to the Middle East, which made Limassol a target for Arab raiders.

The Knights Templar, under the Lusignans, developed Limassol further and it became known for the Commandaria wine produced from the surrounding vineyards which visitors can still enjoy today. However, the prosperity did not last and Limassol was marked by a succession of disasters, both natural and man-made. Firstly it was damaged by earthquakes, then in 1373 it was burned by the Genoese to be followed by a century of Arab raids culminating in total destruction by the Turks in 1539. Visitors to the city gave sad accounts of its state, including one by John Locke who said 'the towne is ruinated and nothing in it worth writing [about]'.

In the nineteenth century its port came into use again and it began to see greater prosperity. Today, Limassol is a major production centre, especially for wine, cement and bricks, many of which are exported in the huge ships that leave from the new port to the west of the town.

Limassol is the island's major wine centre, with several large wineries just outside the town and every September it holds a wine festival. This is only one of several festivals which take place in the town, the most spectacular of which is the spring carnival when decorated floats go through the city as part of ten days of parades and celebration.

There are plenty of hotels and apartment blocks in the town, although as usual it is difficult for the independent traveller to find a room which has not been booked up in advance by the tour companies. Limassol has literally hundreds of restaurants, mainly on the waterfront and in the centre of town.

The town has a complicated one-way system and the main sea-front road is very busy. It is difficult to find anywhere to park. The best place to start is the seafront where there are two municipal car parks.

The bus stations are near the market and at the junction of Irene and Enosis streets. From here it is possible to get buses to Nicosia and Paphos. There are also buses to Platres in the Troodos mountains.

The tourist office is at the far end of the promenade almost opposite the old harbour. The other main municipal buildings: post office, police station and the like, are inland in the shopping area.

The main historical site of interest is the medieval **Limassol Castle** which lies a little inland from the western end of the promenade. The current buildings were completed in the early fourteenth century on the site of an earlier Byzantine construction. Some of the earlier fortifications can be seen just inside the walls. This is where Richard the Lionheart married Berengaria, but the chapel in which the ceremony took place is no longer standing and the central hall collpased in 1523. The Turks took the castle over in 1570 and increased the fortifications and it was then used as a jail. Under British control it was the headquarters of the British forces. Since then it has been restored and it is open to visitors. The entrance is up some steps and to the right is the great hall from where it is possible to go up onto the castle walls which offer good views out over the city.

The castle is in a pleasant area with its own garden and looks out over some of the traditional artist's shops and houses. It now houses the **Cyprus Medieval Museum**. In the basement are photographs of the Byzantine churches of Cyprus, as well as some replicas of sculptures from the Santa Sophia cathedral in northern Nicosia. At the time of writing the spiral steps are not worth ascending as they are blocked off after a couple of flights.

The exhibits on the upper floors are arranged in small rooms off a central hallway. On the ground floor are coats of arms, wall paintings and tombstones, particularly from Nicosia and the church at Pyrga. On the second floor are some impressive displays of weaponry and a full suit of armour. There are also exhibits of jewellery and pottery and some fine stone gargoyles. The stairs up to the next floor lead out to the battlements from where there are good views of the city. Even better views can be found from the next floor which is a small raised square right at the top of the castle.

There are two mosques in the town, both visible from the castle: Djami Djedd, a little to the west and Djami Kebir mosque, reminders that this was once the Turkish part of the town.

On the seafront the old harbour is a quiet place full of yachts and fishing boats. The main shipping business now takes place in the huge new port to the west of the town. The promenade is a reasonably pleasant place although the stony beach is not very impressive.

Inland and parallel to the main promenade is the main shopping area. The best shopping street is Anexartissias, starting beyond the Cyprus handicraft service. There are some good specialist shops selling silver, pottery and leather goods and at the far end of the road

Wine Production in Cyprus

Wine has been produced in Cyprus for 4,000 years. The earliest evidence of this production comes from wine jars found at *Salamis*. The Dionysos mosaic in Paphos also shows the importance of wine and depicts what is claimed to be the first recorded hangover in history.

The first wines were exported by the Lusignans in the twelfth century. In 1363 Peter I visited London to raise funds for the Crusades. The Lord Mayor of London held a banquet for him and four other kings who were toasted in Cyprus wines. The painting of the banquet can be seen in the Royal Exchange in London. Wine production then declined under the Turks for religious reasons.

Today wine is central to the Cypriot economy. 155,000 tons of grapes are produced each year and 5 million gallons of Cyprus wines are exported to the UK alone. Vineyards are found on the southern slopes of the Troodos mountains and in the Limassol and Paphos area. Local people also grow their own vines on trellises in their gardens. Visitors to the island in September will see the grapes being picked and if they are unlucky will be stuck behind one of the extremely slow moving grape lorries taking its load down the mountain to one of the wineries on the coast.There are five main producers of wine in Cyprus and their wineries can be found along the coast in Limassol and Paphos.

One of the most famous wines of Cyprus is Commandaria St John which was first produced by the Knights Hospitaller from their base in Kolossi. It is a sweet dessert wine which is still popular today. Aphrodite white wine and Othello red wine are perhaps the most well known and widely available wines in restaurants and shops. Cyprus also produces sherry, Emva cream and brandy.

is a new shopping precinct.

On Saint Andrew Street (Ayios Andreou), there are more shops including a Marks and Spencer's store. At the far end of the street is the **Folk Art Musuem** which has a collection of national costumes, tapestry and embroidery in a restored house. Next door is the municipal library.

Returning to the seafront promenade, at the far eastern end, are the public gardens which contain flowers and palm trees which are well watered and provide a haven of green among the dust of the city. In spring it is the site of the flower show and in September is the venue for the wine festival. This takes place over twelve days in September and involves drinking, dancing and drama. All the major drink producers set up trade stands around the gardens, along with other traditional hallmarks of a Cypriot festival like the sweet stall selling nuts and well sugared, sticky sweets. A small open-air theatre in the gardens puts on occasional performances during the summer. There is also a small zoo containing the Cyprus moufflon.

The **District Museum** is housed in a modern building just behind the park. It has a pleasant garden containing a sundial which was

Limassol Wine Festival

once owned by Lord Kitchener. Room 1 contains Neolithic tools and pottery covering a huge time span from 3,000BC to 1300 AD from *Amathus*, *Kourion* and Limassol itself. There are six amphorae in one corner from 2,300BC. Room 2 has figurines and jewellery from 1,700BC, Roman coins and even early razor blades. Also of interest is a bronze bull. Room 3 contains some of the most important finds, including statues of the Egyptian god Bes and Artemis found at *Amathus* and some other fragments of statues representing other deities.

Another possible excursion is a visit to the KEO distillery and winery on the west side of the city between the old and new harbour on Franklin Roosevelt Street. Visitors can see the wine being made and take part in wine tasting.

In Limassol itself, the beaches are poor although there are long stretches of sand along the ribbon development to the east of the town. These are masked by the hotels, but there are well marked tracks showing the public access.

Dhassoudi beach just east of the city centre is a public beach run by the tourist organisation. There are many sports facilities in the complex including a swimming pool and tennis courts. It is easy to miss, as it is surrounded by hotels.

The carnival in Limassol takes place just before Lent and lasts ten days, reaching its climax at the weekend when there are singing competitions called Cantades in which rival groups of singers compete with each other. On the last Sunday there is a grand parade of lavishly decorated floats through the town.

THE AKROTIRI PENINSULA

The peninsula contains a salt lake and the airport of the British base of **Akrotiri** which is of central strategic importance. Around the lake is an important agricultural area, known as the Phassouri plantations, where citrus fruits and grapes are grown. There are also a large number of Cypress trees which line the roads in spectacular fashion. It is possible to visit some of the farms; those interested should contact the tourist office. The lake itself, like its counterpart in Larnaca, is a stopping off point for flamingoes.

Lady's Mile is the main beach on the peninsula, and stretches for 5 miles (8 km). It is reached by heading towards the main port and then following the signs to the beach. The road is quite bad in places but improves the further you get from town. The landscape is quite interesting with the flat dustiness of the salt lake on the right and even in summer the visitor will smell the distinctive scent of the salt. The beach itself is long and sandy but the view back to Liamssol of the port is not that impressive. The far end of the beach is closed off by barbed wire behind which is the RAF base of Akrotiri.

Also on the peninsula, reached on a track from the far end of Lady's Mile, following the line of the base, is St Nicholas of the Cats Church. It was founded in 325AD although the curent buildings date from the thirteenth century. It was abandoned in 1570 under the Turkish occupation. Above the north entrance is a marble section dating from the medieval period and depicting four coats of arms. Cats were introduced to control pests, especially snakes, but the cats themselves have now overrun the place. It is occupied today by nuns and visitors can look round, but the nunnery is closed in the early afternoon for siesta.

Additional Information

Accommodation
Camping
Governor's Beach Campsite
13 miles (20km) east of Limassol
☎ 05 632300
247 places
Open: April-October

Youth Hostel
120 Ankara Street
(behind the castle)
☎ 05 363749
Open: 7.30am-11.30pm all year round.

Boats
There are boat trips from Limassol harbour to Lady's Mile beach.

Places to Visit
Amathus Archaeological Site
Spread over a wide area. One of the most easily accessible parts is the tomb in the grounds of the Amathus Beach Hotel. The other is off the main road and contains the *Agora*.

Limassol Castle
Cyprus Medieval Museum
Near the old port
☎ 05 330419

Open: Mon-Sat 7.30am-6pm all year round

Limassol District Archaeological Museum
On corner of Kuningos and Vryonos St near public gardens
☎ 05 330132
Open: May-Sept Mon-Sat 7.30am-6pm, Sun 10am-1pm; Oct-Apr 7.30am-5pm, Sun 10am-1pm

Folk Art Museum
St Andrew Street
☎ 05 362303
Open: May-Sept Mon, Wed, Fri 8.30am-1pm, 4-6pm, Tues, Thurs, Sat 8.30am-1pm; Oct-Apr Mon, Wed, Fri 8.30am-1pm, 3-5pm, Tues, Thurs, Sat 8.30am-1pm

Factory Visits
KEO distillery
Franklin Roosevelt Street
☎ 05 362053
Open normal working hours

Sodap
☎ 05 364605

Loel
☎ 05 369344

The Wine Products Commission will arrange visits
☎ 05 364692

Local Events
Limassol Carnival
February
Parades and celebrations

Limassol Festival
June
The programme includes music, dance and plays. More details of the performances are available from the tourist office.

Limassol Wine Festival
September
A 12-day festival in the municipal gardens with plenty wine and food available.

Sport Facilities
Athletics
There is an athletics stadium 5km (3 miles) north of the town centre where football matches take place.

Fishing
Sea fishing is possible on the coast. Fishing is allowed in the following dams all year round with a licence:
Germasogia Dam (northeast of Limassol)
Polemidhia dam (5 miles, 8km, northwest of Limassol)

Horse Riding
Elias Beach Horse Riding Centre
Limassol-Nicosia road
Open all year, 12.30-3pm

Swimming
There is an Olympic pool next to the Dhassoudi Beach complex.

Shooting
Limassol shooting club
Polemidhia (5 miles, 8km, north-west of the city centre)
Open: 3 days a week

Tennis
Limassol Sporting Club
West of town centre.

There are also tennis courts at Dhassoudi and at many of the major hotels.

Tourist Offices
15 Spyros Araouzas Street
☎ 05 362756
35 George A Street

Opposite Dhassoudi beach
☎ 05 323211
There is also a service for tourists at Limassol harbour.

Transport
To Nicosia: Kemek Bus, corner
    Enosis and Irinis Street
    Costas Bus, 9B Thessalonikis
    Street
To Larnaca: Kallenos Bus, corner
    Arazaous and Hadjipavlou
    Street (seafront)
To Paphos: Kemek Bus Co, corner
    Enosis and Irinis Street
        ☎ 05 363241
Costas Bus, 9B Thessaloniki Street
        ☎ 05 354394
There are also buses to the mountain hill resorts. The tourist office has details.

Entertainment
There are numerous productions of plays in the amphitheatre at *Kourion*. Details from the tourist office. Other plays, music recitals and dance displays take place throughout the May-Sept.

Emergencies
Limassol General Hospital
☎ 05 330333

General emergency ☎ 199

5

LIMASSOL TO PAPHOS

It is in this region that some of the first settlement of the island took place, making it one of the richest in archaeological finds. The main coast road runs along the distinctive white cliffs for much of the route, allowing spectacular views down to the sea. One of the most impressive is that of Petra tou Romiou; this is the site where, according to legend, Aphrodite emerged from the sea. This legend, once established, meant that this part of the island attracted many religious pilgrims which led to more settlement. As a result the area is one of the most interesting to explore and as an additional incentive there are some good beaches as well.

Leaving Limassol, the first site of interest is **Kolossi** castle, 9 miles (14½km) from the town centre. Follow the signs to the port and then turn right at the T-junction just inside the Phassouri plantations where the long tree-lined avenues begin. Alternatively leave Limassol on the Paphos road and turn left at Kolossi village. Originally, the site was the camp of Isaac Comnenos, the self-styled ruler of the island in 1191. He had mistreated Richard the Lionheart who was shipwrecked here and who predictably retaliated, pursuing Comnenos first to Kolossi and then across to the other side of the island where he was captured.

The Lusignans then took over the island and the land around Kolossi was given to the Knights Hospitaller by Hugh I and they probably built the first fort. In 1291, when Acre was captured by the Arabs the Knights moved their headquarters to Kolossi. This was probably the first example of the use of Cyprus as a safe haven from trouble in the Middle East, a role which it has frequently taken on since. About forty villages were controlled by the Grand Commandery of the Knights. The land was extremely fertile and produced sugar cane and vines from which came the famous

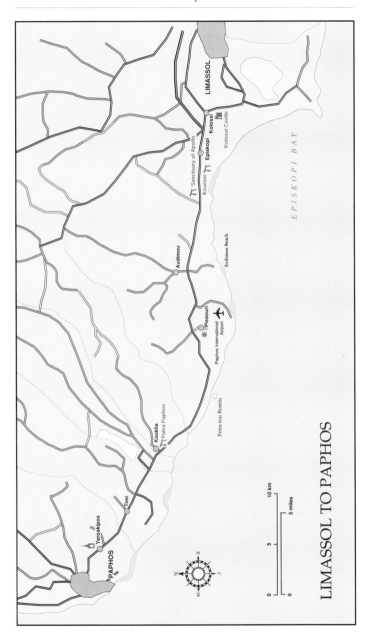

LIMASSOL TO PAPHOS

Commandaria wine, a sweet dessert wine, which is still sold today. The land around the castle remains remarkably productive, staying green even when a virtual dustbowl has hit the rest of the island.

Kolossi was unsuccessfully attacked by the Genoese in both 1373 and 1402 and its lands were attacked by the Mamelukes a few decades later causing extensive damage. The main buildings visible today were the result of rebuilding in the fifteenth century by the Grand Commander Louis de Magnac. They later passed into the Cornaro family and finally the Turks took over the land in 1570.

The castle is set slightly off the road where there is a car park and a small café. It lies in a pleasant garden and visitors enter across the drawbridge. Above the entrance to the keep is a coat of arms of Louis de Magnac. The machicoulis on the outside were used to pour boiling oil onto any attackers. The keep is a very impressive structure with walls 9ft (2.75m) thick and three storeys high. Just inside is a painting of the crucifixion. There are interconnecting vaulted chambers on all three storeys.

The second storey, reached up some spiral steps, has two rooms with large fireplaces. These were the apartments of the Grand Commander and they have four large windows with seats built into them making the rooms very light and airy. A spiral staircase leads to the roof from where there are good views of the surrounding area, including a little brown church in the distance and the aqueduct which used to supply the village with water.

In the basement, also accessible from the moat, are two very dark rooms. Moving out into the pleasant grounds are numerous store-rooms and stables as well as the remains of some of the earlier fortifications. A large vaulted church-like building was used to make sugar; this was a key industry until it was rendered uneconomic by competition from the West Indies. There are also ruins of a mill. The whole castle is a very peaceful place, and refreshingly cool in the midday heat.

To reach the main road again from the castle, head north and then turn left to reach **Episkopi** village, a large settlement with plenty of shops and a mosque. There is also a museum containing various artefacts from *Kourion* (the site is a couple of miles away on the main road). It is kept in a pleasant old house and was started by an American archaeologist. In the first case are terracotta chariots from the sanctuary and on the wall arrowheads. The next case has figurines and other votive objects and on the wall jewellery, coins, and scarab seals.The third case has limestone heads, pottery and carvings. There is also a marble fountain in the form of a lion.

Visitors should note that as the main road begins to climb there are many dangerous bends. The route can also be busy and Cypriot lorries incredibly slow moving. Patience is the only safe option and drivers should not be tempted to imitate the madcap overtaking of their Cypriot counterparts.

There are several beaches accessible on tracks from the main road. However, the main attraction of this region is *Kourion* (*Curium*), one of the most important and impressive archaeological sites on the island. It stands spectacularly above the sea on the cliffs, with a good beach below the site, reached on a track, signed from the road. However, those parts of the beach marked by red buoys are subject to dangerous currents. A short distance uphill is the main access to the ruins where there is a tourist pavilion with a restaurant and a car park. (At the time of writing this entrance, but not the tourist pavilion, is closed and access is further east.)

There is evidence from tombs found near Episkopi village that there has been a settlement in this area since the Neolithic period. The main occupation started with the arrival of the Myceneans and the Dorians. *Kourion* became one of the many City Kingdoms on the island and by 673BC is recorded as being important enough to pay tribute to the Assyrians. At this point the main settlement moved closer to the sea on the Paleokastro bluff and it seems to have adopted the cult of worshipping Apollo, building a sanctuary to him to the west of the city.

It rebelled against the Persians in 498BC but then changed sides during the battle of Salamis to support them. This defection was instrumental in allowing the Persians to take control of the island. *Kourion* remained a significant player in Cypriot politics and later flourished under Roman rule. It was extensively damaged in the earthquakes of the fourth century. Like all the coastal cities it was ravaged by Arab raids during the seventh century with the result that it had to be abandoned as its population moved inland. During the Venetian period the area was under the control of the Cornaro family and became very prosperous.

The first excavations of the site took place in 1873. They were undertaken by Cesnola, the American consul of the period who managed to convince the administration that he should be allowed to dig where he wished across the island; a decision much lamented by later archaeologists who followed in his somewhat destructive wake. During these excavations he discovered the *Curium* treasure, a collection of gold and silver objects which were sold to the Metropolitan Museum in New York.

At the time of writing only the *Theatre* and the *Basilica* are open to the public, the rest are closed off to the public while further excava-

⇐ *Kolossi castle*

The Roman Theatre at Kourion

The Basilica, Kourion

tion takes place but are likely to be reopened and are therefore described here. The first point of interest when the site is fully open is the *Building of the Achilles Mosaic*. This was clearly an important building constructed around a courtyard in which there is a mosaic of Achilles disguised as a woman but inadvertently revealing his identity to Odysseus. A smaller mosaic in an adjoining room shows Ganymede being carried to Olympus by an eagle. This was probably the reception area for visitors and built about 4AD. Following along the road is the *House of the Gladiators*. This too has a mosaic, which shows two gladiators in combat.

The remains of an aqueduct are not far away. This was built by the Romans to bring water from a distant spring and passed over the city walls into the *Fountain House* where it was stored for public use.

Beyond the *Fountain House* on the opposite side of the track is the *Basilica*. It was built in the fifth century, and it is 230ft (70m) long and 133ft (40m) wide with traces of mosaic visible on the floor. It must have once been an impressive structure supported on twelve columns and the stumps of some of these are still visible.

A good 10 minute walk away is the *Theatre*. This is perhaps the most memorable feature of the site, standing in a semicircle with seats for an audience of 3,500. It was probably built by the early Greeks and then extended by the Romans. The seating was also moved back in order to protect it from the animals who were brought in to fight the gladiators. It was first excavated in 1949-50 and rebuilt in 1960. Today it is the venue for concerts and plays during the summer; the tourist office can provide a programme of events.

Up the hill beyond the *Theatre* is the *Annexe of Eustolios*. This was a palace or large villa. It has a well preserved mosaic floor which bears the invocation, 'enter and good luck to the house'. The villa is built around a courtyard with porticoes on three sides and visitors walk round on raised gangways. On the left of the entrance were the servant's quarters and the corridor leads into the courtyard which once had a pool surrounded by mosaics and an inscription which refers to Apollo and to Eustolios who built the *Baths*.

Some steps lead further up the hill to the *Baths*. These also have mosaic floors. The central room has four exceptionally fine panels. The first and most famous shows a partridge, the second a bust of Ktisis, a deity who personified the Creation. From the central room one enters the *Frigidarium* (cold bath) followed by the *Tepidarium* and the *Caldarium* (hot baths). Some of the baths can still be seen along with the mechanism for heating the water and the air ducts and furnaces. A large tank outside supplied the water for the baths which in turn was supplied by the aqueduct.

The site extends much further and to reach the next area of interest visitors need to return to the main road and travel about ¾ mile (1km) towards Paphos and then turn inland. This is the *Stadium* and the shape of the arena is still discernible, as are the entrance gates. Some of the seating has been reconstructed by the excavators, however there is still not much for the amateur to see apart from to marvel at the size of the place. There once were seven tiers of seats which could have held 6,000 spectators. It was built in the second century and remained in use for about four centuries.

Further along the Paphos road, about 2 miles (3km) from the main site is the *Sanctuary of Apollo Hylates* and much more spectacular than the *Stadium*. This was one of the most important religious sites in ancient Cyprus. Apollo, the God of the Woodland, was protector of *Kourion* and was worshipped here from the eighth century BC. It stayed in use until the fourth century although it was rebuilt several times and the existing remains are from about 100 AD when it was reconstructed after an earthquake.

Visitors enter on a marked pathway where there is a map; it is best to try and follow a clockwise circular route. The first points of interest are the steps of the display hall and old *Paphos Gate* and then the circular structure of a votive pit. This is where the priests used to put unwanted ritual gifts and such pits are a very rich source of archaeological finds. The narrow paved road then leads to the *Temple of Apollo*, part of which has now been restored and is especially impressive if the pylons behind it are ignored. Most of the rituals probably took place outside as the temple itself is quite small.

Visitors should then retrace their steps to the covered shed which was the *Priest's House*. Here through the fence, the remains of a mosaic can be seen as well as some pillars. The paved route then passes along the portico of the South Building and then down a flight of steps to the *Palaestra*. This central court was used for athletics and the site has plenty of facilities for sportsmen, including another complex of baths. Next to the *Palaestra* were the dormitories, parts of which are quite well preserved.

Immediately west of the site is the British base of **Episkopi** which is striking for its well watered, green playing fields down in the valley. Episkopi is one of the sovereign bases granted to Britain under the Independence agreement. The bases seem very much a part of England and are seen as an extremely popular posting by the troops sent here. It is usually possible to drive through the base without any checks although occasionally there are security alerts when the checkpoints are used more extensively. The side roads into the base itself are sealed off to the casual visitor by barbed wire.

Drivers should beware on the tight bends leading down the hill into the base.

Three miles further west is the turning to **Evdimou** beach, 17 miles (27km) from Limassol and 2 miles (3km) from the main road on a very narrow track. This is a really good long beach with a sandy shore and pleasant swimming, although the water does become deep quickly. There is a small café and a jetty at the eastern end. Inland, on the other side of the main road is Evdimou village which was an important city in Lusignan and Venetian times. According to legend it was built for Arsinoe by her brother Ptolemy Philaldelphus, in the brief Egyptian period of rule.

Prior to the Turkish invasion it was one of several settlements in the area with a majority Turkish Cypriot population. When it was abandoned by them as they moved north, it was resettled by Greek Cypriot refugees.

The next place of interest is **Pissouri**, both the village and the beach. Visitors from Limassol will reach the beach first, it is sign-posted from the main road and is a pleasant stretch of sand. The village is on the clifftop at a height of 800ft (245m), and is reached on a narrow, winding road and consists of a maze of streets perched on the hill. It has several places which rent rooms; the Bunch of Grapes restaurant offers traditional food in a pleasant setting and claims to be famous throughout Cyprus.

From Pissouri the road reaches some of the spectacular white cliffs of this part of the coast. The route is winding and narrow and the slow Cypriot lorries can be a major irritant.

It is, in any case, not long before one of the most well known and photographed sights on the island is reached and where almost everyone will want to slow down or stop. This is **Petra tou Romiou** (the Rock of Aphrodite), which consists of two large rocks in the sea set against the white cliffs above and the turquoise of the Mediterranean below. The best place for panoramic photographs is on the final bend above the rocks coming from Limassol, those travelling the other way will have to look back or stop, although there are some reasonable vantage points on the Paphos side of the rocks.

According to legend, Aphrodite was born here, emerging from the sea and becoming a kind of patron saint of the island. The beach is shingly but the setting spectacular. The scene has been a source of inspiration for many poets and painters, the most famous result being Boticelli's *Birth of Venus*. It is also known for its association with a legendary Cypriot giant Dighenis Akritas who kept Arab pirates at bay by throwing rocks at them from the hillside above.

Up on the cliffs is a tourist pavilion with a restaurant and good views of the rocks below. There is also a car park just off the road and what claims to be a service station. The beach is reached through an underpass, which it is sensible to use, as otherwise pedestrians have to take their chance on a dangerous bend.

About 6 miles (9½km) away, where the land becomes brown and flatter, is the turning to the village of **Kouklia** and the major archaeological site of *Palea Paphos* (old Paphos) as distinct from the site of the modern town, Nea Paphos (new Paphos), 10 miles (16km) further west. It is also signposted as the Sanctuary of Aphrodite. The main site lies on a flat area on top of a hill. The city was probably built by the Arcadian king Agapenor, who stopped here on his way back from Troy. The first settlement was in 1,500BC and grew into an important city. It drew the focus of the Persian attack in 498BC when the Paphians were defeated.

It was known as a sanctuary of Aphrodite because, after having emerged from the sea at Petra Tou Romiou she was brought here and a temple established which attracted a large number of pilgrims. The area flourished until about 321BC when the site at Nea Paphos grew up and a rivalry emerged between the two cities and *Palea Paphos* lost its supremacy, although it remained important for its sanctuary.

Petra tou Romiou, where Aphrodite is said to have been born from the sea

Pilgrims from all over the Roman world, including several emperors, came here on festival days marching from Nea Paphos to the site, accompanied by music and grand decoration of myrtle (the plant associated with Aphrodite). At this time several Roman public buildings were added to the site.

During the Christian period the city's pagan origins seem to have counted against it and it declined further. In the thirteenth century the Lusignans built a castle (Chateau de Covocle) here, from where they controlled the extensive sugar plantations. It was destroyed by Mameluke raids in 1426 but was rebuilt and used by the Turkish Chiftlik, the local governor. The manor house has been restored and is used as a museum, although of the earlier medieval building only the east and south wing survive. The Turks built their own north and west wings and used the place as a farmhouse. The parts of the building which have been restored are inhabited by local families.

The museum is reached up some steps to a large hall 98ft (30m) long with small windows. From here there are good views of the surrounding countryside. There is a history of the excavation of the site and fragments of mosaic. The prize exhibit is the black conical stone which was the manifestation of Aphrodite which the pilgrims worshipped. There are also fragments of rock with inscriptions dedicated to Aphrodite, a huge stone jar, various figurines and an ancient bathtub. In the central case are various weapons and around the walls limestone statues from the siege ramp. Other exhibits from the medieval period, include pots and cauldrons.

To the east of the museum, is the *Sanctuary of Aphrodite*, built around a central courtyard. This is where the rituals would have taken place. The goddess was not represented in human form but by the conical stone which was annointed with oil. In front of the manor house are several buildings associated with the temple consisting of two colonnaded halls. Around the court are several chambers which are a mixture of early construction and later Roman additions.

The south wing is the best preserved part of this building and the remaining walls are still quite high, made of blocks up to 7ft (2.1m) in height. There was possibly a Phoenecian temple inside this wing in a small courtyard, but once again Roman reconstruction has added to the confusion of the original layout.

West of the sanctuary are Roman remains including a large Roman Peristyle House built in 1AD. It consists of rooms around a colonnaded atrium and contains mosaics. The house was possibly a residence for the priests who tended the sanctuary. There are ruins of several other Roman houses on the site, most notably the house of Leda. This is reached on a marked path, and contains a copy of the mosaic depicting Leda and the swan.

There are also remains of the Christian period including the Katholiki church which is inside a small cloister and close to the temple. It dates from the Byzantine period when it served the village and has some wall paintings; unfortunately most are very faded.

Also on the site, ¾ mile (400m) to the northeast of Kouklia, is Marcello Hill, the northeast gate and the siege works. These were the extensive defences of the site which were gradually added to and strengthened as the city was attacked by different enemies. The walls stand only about 3ft (1m) high but the impressive arrangments are still visible. The road through the walls is very narrow and turns in a sharp bend. Marks on the walls show how the wheels of vehicles failed to cope with the narrow entrance. The gate was once 41ft (12.5m) wide with a bastion on either side, but when the defences were strengthened the entrance was narrowed to 9.2ft (2.8m) and guard rooms added.

The siege ramp, outside the gate, was built by the Persians when they attacked the city in 498BC. Archaeologists have worked out how this operation was meant to work and how it was thwarted by the defenders. The Persians attacked and destroyed the sanctuary. They then used the ruins, soil and trees to build the ramp up against the city wall. This has proved an exceptionally rich source of artefacts for the archaeologists who have found objects ranging from fragments of columns to sculptures and a sculpted head of a priest-king.

Most of the ramp has now been removed and some artefacts placed in the musuem on the main site. The defenders dug tunnels beneath the city walls to try and topple the towers being used by the enemy to attack the city. The tunnels were up to 7.6ft (2.3m) high and were lit by ancient lamps and supported by timbers which were then set on fire. This formed a furnace effect, causing the ramp to collapse. One of the tunnels is still preserved. However, this ingenuity seems to have had little success, for after fierce fighting — testified to by the large number of arrowheads found here — the city was captured.

Rejoining the main Paphos road one reaches **Timi** village and below it Timi beach. This is close to the international airport and is noisy when the jets take off, but as Paphos is not that busy an airport this need not be a serious drawback.

More beaches can be found at **Yeroskipos** (Geroskipou) where there is a public beach run by the tourist organisation with a restaurant, changing facilities and water sports. The beach is 2 miles (3km) below the village, or reached from Paphos on the coast road which passes all the new hotels which have their own mediocre stretches of sand. There are also shingly stretches beyond the tourist beach,

heading towards the campsite.

Yeroskipos village is not a particularly distinguished place and its main street is very busy as it doubles as the Limassol to Paphos road, but the square near the church is picturesque. The village is noted for two things, its church and its Cyprus delight shops (known as Turkish delight in less sensitive times). The church of Ayia Paraskevi is Byzantine and dates from the tenth century. It is one of the most attractive on the island and is also one of the most unusual, having five domes. The three domes over the nave intersect with two over the aisles to form a cross. Some of the decorations over the altar date from the nineth century. Most of the paintings are of a later period, including a twelfth-century depiction of the Dormition of the Virgin Mary. Most of the frescoes in the nave are from the fifteenth century; note especially the unusual picture of the Virgin Mary.

The village also has an excellent folk art museum, set back from the main road in an eighteenth-century Cypriot house, which was occupied in Victorian times by the British vice-consul. The ground

A traditional Cypriot weaving loom in the Folk Art Museum, Yeroskipos

⇐ *Springtime in Yeroskipos*

floor contains farming and domestic tools ranging from bread cutters to tongs to catch eels. Upstairs are traditional costumes and pottery, while outbuildings include local trades and industries.

The remainder of the village consists of a few restaurants and a profusion of Cyprus delight shops. Several of these offer visitors the chance to watch the sweet being made. From here one begins to enter the outskirts of the modern town of Paphos.

Additional Information

Accommodation
Camping
Yeroskipou Zenon Gardens
½ mile east of the tourist beach
PO Box 99
☎ 06 242277
Open: March to October
95 places

Youth Hostel
37 Eleftherios Venizelos Avenue
Paphos
☎ 06 232588
Open: all year 7.30-10am, 4-11pm

Places to Visit
Kourion Archaeological Site
(off the Limassol to Paphos road)
Open: May-Sept 7.30am-7.30pm,
Oct-Apr 7.30am to sunset

Kourion Museum
Episkopi village
Open: May-Sept Mon- Sat 7.30am-
1.30pm; Oct-Apr Mon-Fri 7.30am-
2pm, Sat 7.30am-1pm

Palea Paphos Archaeological Site
Kouklia
(off the Limassol to Paphos road)
Open: May-Sept 7.30am-7.30pm,
Oct-Apr 7.30am to sunset

Sanctuary of Apollo
2 miles west of Kourion
Open: May-Sept 7.30am-7.30pm,
Oct-Apr 7.30am to sunset

Folk Art Museum
Yeroskipos
☎ 04 630169
Open: May-Sept Mon-Sat 7.30am-
1.30pm; Oct-Apr Mon-Fri 7.30am-
pm, Sat 7.30am-1pm

Kolossi Castle
Open: daily May-Sept 7.30am-
7.30pm, Oct-Apr 7.30am until
sunset

Petra tou Romiou
Tourist pavilion on the cliffs above
the rocks.

Transport
To Kolossi from Limassol: bus no
    16 from Limassol Bus station
To *Kourion* from Limassol or
    Paphos; take the Limassol to
    Paphos Kemek Bus and ask the
    driver to stop

Entertainment
Throughout the May-Sept there are
frequent performances of Classical
drama both Greek and European at
Kourion. Details available from the
tourist offices.

Emergencies
Limassol Hospital
☎ 05 330333

Paphos Hospital
☎ 06 232364.

General emergency ☎ 199

6

PAPHOS

For a period in Classical times, Paphos was the capital of the island and one of the most significant City Kingdoms. However, its position so far west on the island means that it has spent much of its history as a remote outpost, ill served by transport links. Then, when the airport was built just outside the town it began a rapid transformation into a holiday resort with all the usual tourist paraphernalia. Although it remains the smallest town on the island with a population of 23,000, it is one of the most interesting to explore.

The Paphos one sees today is Nea (new) Paphos which distinguishes it from *Palea* (old) *Paphos*, the historical site down the road. It is thought that the new city was founded in the fourth century BC by King Nikokles as a port for the older city, although there are claims that it was founded much earlier by Agapenor who led the Arcadians in the Trojan war and was diverted here in a storm. It was besieged by the Ptolemies in 312BC and legend has it that Nikokles, rather than face defeat, committed suicide by burning down the palace.

Under the Ptolemies (Egyptians) the town then became an important centre and even minted its own coins. The Roman period saw further prosperity and the town had the first Christian governor who was converted, after initial resistance, by St Paul and St Barnabas. By the first century BC it had taken over from *Salamis* as the island's capital.

The town then suffered extensive damage in a series of earthquakes and its influence declined as power was transferred back to *Salamis*. Paphos remained in ruins for many years, although it did help to supply Crusader ships during the medieval period and was known for its shipbuilding. Like all the coastal towns it suffered at the hands of Arab raiders and this seems to have been the reason for

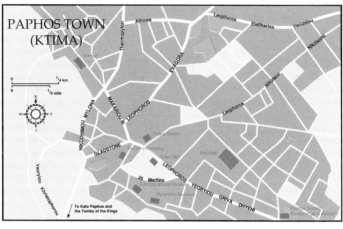

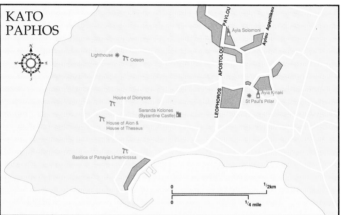

the creation of the upper town, the Ktima area.

Modern Paphos is divided into two parts. Around the harbour is called **Kato Paphos** (lower Paphos) and the upper town, **Ktima**. These used to be clearly separated but now so much development has taken place that the division is no longer clear, it is however a long walk between the two centres. Ktima contains most of the shops and the cheaper hotels and is less oriented for the tourist, whereas Kato Paphos has the luxury hotels and main tourist facilities.

There are some rooms to rent and cheaper hotels in Paphos, but finding accommodation at the height of the season is still a problem.

The market in Paphos upper town is a good place to meet the Cypriots

The harbour and fort, Kato Paphos

As usual there are plenty of restaurants around the harbour. The tourist office is up in the Ktima part of town on Gladstone Street. Parking is reasonably easy near the harbour, less so in the upper town although there is a huge new municipal car park on the way into the shopping area. Traffic is very heavy around the upper town, especially in the late afternoon.

Most visitors will start their exploration of Paphos on the seafront. At the far eastern, Yeroskipos, end are the large luxury hotels which have reasonable beaches. If visitors are in Paphos in September they might like to visit the the SODAP winery which lies between these hotels and those of Paphos proper. At that time of year, lorries full of grapes struggle down from the mountains and line up in the winery yard to unload their contents.

West of the winery are some more large hotels and various tourist shops which, it has to be said do not show Cyprus off at its best. The main products are lurid T-shirts and pirate videos, however there are a few better handicrafts shops set back from the road. The town beach is not very impressive, just a small patch of sand in between the rocks. There are better beaches by the main hotels or visitors can take a trip out to the Yersokipos tourist beach just outside the town or up the west coast to Coral Bay. There are frequent buses to these beaches which call at the main hotels.

The harbour area is, however, a much more pleasant place lined with cafés enlivened by the most famous resident of Paphos: the pelican which wanders along the seafront having its photograph taken and which has provided the motif for many of the cafés. The bird does seem a little shyer than in recent years and there is no guarantee that he will appear.

Halfway along the seafront behind the Pelican café is an early Christian Basilica, **Panayia Limeniotissa** (Our Lady of the Harbour), built in the fifth century. It lies in ruins now but its ground plan can be made out. It had three aisles divided by rows of columns and the floor used to be covered in mosaics. The site is locked up and visitors will have to peer through the fence.

The harbour is still used by small fishing boats. There are also various boat trips out to Lara's wonderful beaches as well as to a nearby shipwreck in a glass-bottomed boat. There are numerous cafés along the side of the harbour which are pleasant places to stop.

At the far end of the harbour is **Paphos Fort** or rather forts. There are ruins of one fort on the breakwater, but these consist only of two lumps of rock. A second better preserved structure was built by the Lusignans. It was dismantled by the Venetians to stop the Turks taking it over and using it against them. However, when the Turks invaded they restored it for use as a prison. The castle is in a very pleasant setting and is reached across a drawbridge. Today it is possible to visit the interior and see the dungeons, as well as climb up to the walls and look out over the city.

Behind the harbour are all the archaeological sites. They are encircled by the city wall which can be followed round for most of its length, although it is best preserved on its northwestern edge where it was cut out of the rock. The walls enclose the site of Nea Paphos which covers an area of 1.1 million square yards (950,000sq m) and stretches from the harbour in the south to the lighthouse at the northern end. Some of the site is on open land, the rest lies in between the houses of Kato Paphos where the visitor can stumble upon ancient temples, theatres and churches.

The best way to tour the archaeological sites it is take the signed road off Apostolou Pavlou Avenue. The first site contains the remains of the Byzantine castle. It is also known as '**Saranda Kolones**' (forty columns) after the columns which were found on the site and which can still be seen. The castle was probably built in the seventh century as protection against Arab raiders. It had an outer wall which was some 10ft (3m) thick and a moat. The square keep was built around a courtyard and had substantial towers at each corner. Entry was through a fifth gate tower on the east side. Although the building is in ruins there are many fragments of towers and dungeons to explore, but all are unprotected and those with small children should be careful on the higher parts of the ruins.

Further up the road are perhaps the most impressive remains found in Paphos: the mosaics, the finest in the Eastern Mediterranean. These are now protected all on one site in three houses. The first is the **House of Dionysos**, where the mosaics were discovered by a farmer ploughing his field and excavations began in 1962. Visitors walk along raised platforms to look down on the mosaics.

Turning clockwise along the outer platforms are mosaics showing the figure of a man, various patterns of shapes, and a depiction of a peacock. At the back of the house is one of the best known — a depiction of Ganymede being taken back to Olympus by an eagle. They are very well preserved, especially the natural colours of the limestone. In the inner series, in the *Atrium*, there are four panels, mainly depicting hunting scenes. In the first is a picture of Pyramus and Thisbe, the second Dionysos and Ikarios, the third Poseidon and Amymone and in the fourth Apollo and Daphne. All show scenes of wine drinking.

The most famous mosiac, depicted on a thousand postcards, is that of the triumph of Dionysos with the God in a chariot drawn by leopards. Behind him are a gathering of followers engaged in various revelries. According to legend Dionysos was the first man to discover how to make wine and he taught the technique to Ikarios (shown in the mosiac) who in turn let his shepherds into the secret. They drank too much and thought that they had been poisoned and turned on Ikarios bringing about his tragic end. The remaining mosaics show numerous hunting scenes depicting a wide range of animals, including tigers.

At the other side of the site, on a marked path is the **House of Aion**. This contains mosaics uncovered in 1983. The five scenes, although partially damaged are of superb quality. In the top left is a depiction of Leda and Zeus in the form of a swan. The top right panel shows Dionysos as a baby accompanied by various nymphs. The middle panel shows a beauty contest between sea nymphs, of which Aion is the judge. At the bottom of the mosaic is the triumphant procession of Dionysos and the final picture shows Apollo punishing a foolish man who had challenged the God to a musical duel and lost.

Passing the ongoing excavation, the visitor reaches the **House of Theseus** named after its principal mosaic showing Theseus killing

The Byzantine castle of Saranda Kolones, Paphos

the minotaur. The house is built around a courtyard and some of the wings are still to be excavated. All the rooms had mosaics but many of these have not been preserved. The best are in the south wing where the Thesesus mosaic is alongside one showing the birth of Achilles. The first shows Theseus surrounded by a personification of Crete and Ariadne who helped him slay the minotaur by giving him the thread which allowed him to escape from the Labyrinth. The second shows Achilles being washed by his mother and father, Thetis and Peleus, with the three Fates in the background. The house probably belonged to a Roman governor.

Descending from the mosaics, visitors should take the road to the modern lighthouse. The lighthouse is not open to the public but there are good views from the path leading to it and some remote rocky beaches below. The rocky mound is thought to have been the *Acropolis* of the town where there was once a temple, although little of this has survived. Just east of the *Acropolis* is the **Odeon**, in a fenced site with free access. The *Theatre* has been partly restored after excavation. It is a semicircle with a stage and twelve rows of seats visible. It was built in the second century AD but was damaged in the

The lighthouse and Roman Theatre, Paphos

earthquake and abandoned in the seventh century.

The *Agora*, a large court (1,000sq ft, 95sq m) used as a market place, stands in front of the *Odeon*. Only the foundations and parts of the columns are visible. It probably dates from the second century. South of the *Odeon* is a collection of buildings which served as an *Asklepion* (shrine of the god of healing, Asklepeios). None of these are easily discernible.

Returning to the main town and Apostolou Pavlou Avenue the main site of interest is that of the church of **Ayia Kiriaki** (where both Roman Catholic and Anglican services are held each Sunday) and St Paul's Pillar. It is reached from the avenue along Stilis Ag Pavlou Street. The roads are quite confusing, simply try to keep heading east, initially following the signs to the 'Steak House'.

On the fenced site are several granite columns and other fragments of ruins. Archaeologists are not sure which building all these columns belonged to, although one theory is that the site used to be a Roman *Forum*. There is one pillar standing up at the far side of the site which is called **St Paul's Pillar**. Here, according to legend, St Paul was bound and given thirty-nine lashes as a punishment for preaching Christianity. However, despite this he managed to convert the governor to his point of view.

East of the pillar are the remains of yet another church. It was built in 1300 and was refurbished two hundred years later. A large number of Italian sculptures were added and several of these were uncovered during the excavations along with fragments of paintings. It was turned into a mosque by the Turks, but later it collapsed and was abandoned until excavations took place.

Next to this and below Ayia Kiriaki are the remains of one of the earliest Christian basilicas, measuring 164ft (50m) by 125ft (38m). It was a five-aisled edifice and used to be covered in mosaics. The roof was supported on pink granite columns, the remains of which are still visible. Excavation of the area is still going on.

Other sites of interest are found heading up to the old town of Ktima, where just inside the city wall are some underground chambers cut out of the rock called **Garrison's Camp**. They resemble other chambers found at nearby sites and could have been cut in the fourth century BC. The northern and western sides have been excavated and were possibly the living quarters of the soldiers. The site runs off a long corridor with chambers to the east and north. It was probably some sanctuary to a pagan deity but there is no definitive evidence of this and there was also a Christian basilica in the forecourt which is still being excavated.

A little further east is **Fabrica Hill** at the end of Apostolou Pavlou

Avenue. It is a rocky mound where there are more chambers cut out of the rock but it is unclear what they were used for. They had vaulted roofs and possibly painted walls. Just east of here is a large *Theatre* which has not yet been excavated, but there is a good view from the hill to the town and the sea below. An inscription found in the area suggests that it was built in 3BC.

There are two catacombs in the area. The first is that of **Ayia Solomoni**, easily visible from the road due to the tree decorated by handkerchiefs and other items of clothing, left by those who believe in the miraculous curative powers of the catacombs. The church consists of a complex of underground chambers around an open court and was probably used as some kind of refuge. It was altered in Byzantine times when one of the chambers was made into a chapel with numerous frescoes. Some were destroyed by the graffiti of early crusaders who scratched their names on the walls. There is a Holy Well in which the excavators found a large amount of medieval pottery. The catacomb is quite dark but is still used as a church with an altar and an icon in one of the chambers.

There is a second catacomb, **Ayios Lamprianos**, a short distance up the road. This is larger but less impressive as it tends to be rubbish strewn.

In the upper town of Paphos, are the main museums. The first is off Apostolou Pavlou Avenue; turn right off the main road passing various colonial-style government buildings and then right again at the roundabout to reach the **Byzantine Museum**. It has a small collection of religious works, icons and carvings. Behind the musuem is the courtyard of the Bishopric with arched cloisters and a modern church in the centre.

Close by, just across the road, and well signposted, is the **Ethnographical Museum**. This is a private collection which was gathered together by George Eliades and consists of coins, pottery and axeheads along with various kitchen implements. One room contains the reconstruction of a bridal chamber with traditional costumes and furniture. The garden contains two third-century BC tombs, an olive press and a traditional *kleftiko* oven.

On the hill below the Axiothea Hotel is a small park with some catacombs and remnants of statues.

The actual shopping area of Paphos is quite small, and is found at the top of the hill above the large muncipal car park, and consists of several narrow streets which can be very busy. There is one pleasant pedestrianised street which has shops and cafés. Close by, near Agora street is the market which is a colourful lively place where villagers bring their produce to sell. It is only open in the mornings.

The **Paphos District Archaeological Museum**, on the road which leads out of town to the airport and Limassol, is continually expanding as the finds from continuing excavations are added to the collection. In the hall is a Hellenistic sarcophagus which comes from Peyia. Room 1 has rings, pottery, terracotta figures and idols from Lemba and red vases from Polis. There are also examples of Roman pottery and in the wall cases is jewellery. In the middle of the room is a skeleton from the site at Lemba. Room 2 has pottery in classical Greek style, various sculptures and a fine display of coins minted by the various City Kingdoms.

Room 3 contains several sarcophagi and various Roman curiosities including marble eyeballs and clay hot water bottles. The hot water bottles displayed against a human figure were fashioned in the shape of the part of the body to which they were applied, presenting the extraordinary spectacle of hand, feet and even ear-shaped bottles. There are also a wide range of statues of Greek gods, some pretty Roman vases and some rather comical clay face masks. Room 4 displays some small statues and artefacts from the House of Dionysos site, with large jars and a fifth- or sixth-century mosaic on

Ayia Kiriaki and the ruins of the Christian basilica, Paphos

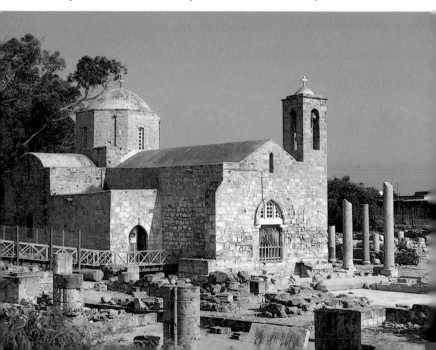

Tombs of the Kings, Paphos, built in the third century BC

the wall. Room 5 has exhibits from later periods, mainly medieval pottery and at the time of writing is being reorganised.

Just outside Paphos is another very impressive site: the **Tombs of the Kings** complex. Those travelling by car should take the road signed to Coral Bay. It seems that no actual royalty was buried here but the tombs were so named because of their impressive size. There are 100 tombs on the site which spreads all across the headland. The most impressive are built around a courtyard with the tombs cut out of the rock and visitors walk around the top and should take care as the drop down into the tombs is a steep one. They can descend down steps to explore further, often encountering a maze of passageways. The tombs in the centre of the site can be a little crowded when the tourist buses are present, but those at the edges of the site are just as impressive and less visited. The tombs are in a Doric style with Doric columns forming a temple façade. They were probably cut in the third century BC.

Additional Information

Accommodation
Lists of hotels are available from the tourist office

Camping
Yeroskipou Zenon Gardens
PO Box 99
☎ 06 242277
Open: March-October
1½ miles (2km) from Paphos harbour on coast road or 1km from the centre of Yeroskipou village. 95 places

Youth Hostel
37 Eleftherias Venizelos Avenue
☎ 06 232588
Open: all year 7.30-10.00am, 4-11pm

Boat Trips
There are boat trips from Paphos Harbour to Coral Bay and Lara

Place to Visit
Tombs of the Kings
(1 mile from centre of Paphos on the road to Coral Bay)
Open: May-Sept 7.30am-7.30pm; Oct-Apr 7.30am- sunset

House of Theseus
House of Dionysos
House of Aion
(on hill above harbour)
Open: May-Sept 7.30am-7.30pm; Oct-Apr 7.30am- sunset

Byzantine Museum
25 March Street
☎ 06 232092
Open; May-Sept Mon-Fri 9am-1pm, 4pm-6pm,Sat 9am-1pm; Oct-Apr 9am-1pm 3pm- 5pm, Sat 9am-1pm

Ethnographical Museum
1 Exo Vrisy Street
Open: May-Sept Mon-Sat 9am-1pm, 4-7pm; Oct-Apr 9am-1pm, 3-5pm

Paphos Archaeological Museum
Dighenis Street
☎ 06 240215
Open: May-Sept Mon-Sat 7.30am-1.30pm, 4-6pm, Sun 10am-1pm; Oct-Apr Mon-Fri 7.30am- 2pm, 3-5pm, Sat 7.30am-1pm, 3-5pm, Sun 10am-1pm

Fort
Open: May-Sept Mon-Sat 7.30am-1.30pm, Oct-Apr 7.30am-2.30pm

SODAP Winery
Contact the tourist office

Local Events
Epiphany (Jan 6th)
In common with other coastal towns Epiphany in Paphos is celebrated by throwing a cross into the sea.

Paphos Carnival
50 days before Easter

Kites Festival
February

The Paphos Cultural Festival
Throughout September, further details from the tourist office

Saint's days are also celebrated throughout Cyprus. St Peter and St Paul are associated with Paphos and their days are celebrated on 28-29 June

Sports
Fishing
Asprokremnos Dam
10 miles (16 km) east of Paphos.
Mavrokolymbos
7 miles (11km) northwest of Paphos.

Riding
Paphos Riding Centre
Tomb of the Kings

Sailing
Paphos Nautical Club
Paphos Port
☎ 06 233745/06 32407

Shooting
Paphos Shooting Club
Anatoliko (12km, 8 miles, east of Paphos)
Open: Wed & Sat 4pm to dusk, Sun 9am to dusk

Swimming
Yeroskipos tourist beach
(1½miles, 2km, east of the town)
There are also tennis courts as part of the complex

Tourist Offices
3 Gladstone Street
Paphos
☎ 06 232841

Paphos Airport
☎ 06 236833
Limited tourist service

Transport
Main Bus Station:
Paphos 'Pervola' Bus station
Thermopyles Street
Paphos

There are no bus services to the airport

Buses to Limassol: Kemek Bus Co, Leontiou St, ☎ 06 234255
Nicosia via Limassol: Costas Bus, 2b Nicodimos Mylona (near post office) ☎ 06 241717. The bus will also pick up pre-booked passengers from their hotels.
Larnaca via Limassol, no direct service
To Polis: Amoroza Bus Co, 79 Pallikarides Street
To Coral Bay: ALEPA bus no 15 stops at all the major hotels. Runs every day, every 30 minutes but less frequent in the middle of the day.

Entertainment
Organised entertainment tends to be in the hotels although there are nightclubs in Ktima Paphos

Emergencies
Paphos General hospital
☎ 06 232364

General emergency ☎ 199

7

WESTERN CYPRUS

This part of the island contains some of its most remote and beautiful areas. Much of the far northwest is inaccesible except by boat but development is taking place at Coral Bay and Polis. The area is now the focus of a conflict between those who wish to expand that development further and those who wish to conserve the area in its natural state and controversy rages over the proposed creation of a national park in the Akamas peninsula.

The West Coast

There are two routes which head north out of Paphos, the first takes a slight detour away from the coast into the hills to the villages of Lemba and Kissonerga. These villages are beginning to cater for tourists with a few shops and cafés. There are numerous archaeological sites in the area. The first is at **Lemba** which is one of the oldest sites on the island where some Neolithic houses have been found. They are circular with a diameter of 28ft (8.5m) and made out of mud and reeds. The roof was conical and supported by a pole planted in the centre of the structure. Various stone and bone tools were found inside the houses. The excavators also found a grave with the bodies of twenty children.

Excavations are continuing both at this site and at **Kissonerga**, a short distance up the coast. A large number of steatite figures have been found at Kissonerga, these small statues both male and female (14in, 36cm high) were used in religious rituals. No structures have been found at Kissonerga but numerous artefacts, including early pottery, were found in depressions carved out of the ground. The road beyond Kissonerga descends quickly to rejoin the coastal route.

The second route, the coast road, signed to Coral Bay from Paphos, runs past many beaches, new hotels and then later extensive banana

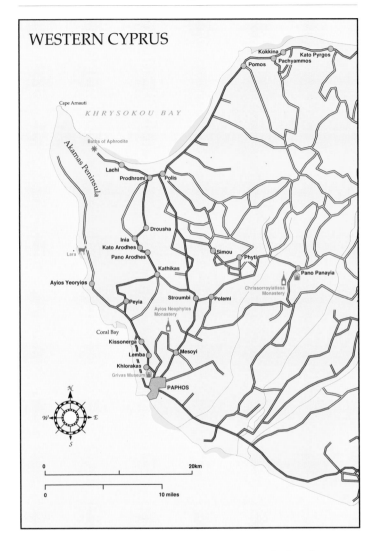

plantations. The road passes below **Khlorakas**, which is famous as the landing site of Colonel Grivas Dhigenis in 1954 at the start of his guerilla campaign against the British and is known as Dhigenis's landing. Dighenis was a Greek god and the name given as a *nom de guerre* to Grivas. There is a small museum here which contains his boat *Ayios Yeoryios* which was captured in 1955 while carrying arms for EOKA. The museum seems to be open and freely accessible all day. The site is almost on the beach below a domed church.

Turn left 8 miles (13km) from Paphos to reach **Coral Bay**, really two bays in the cliffs with a fine beach. This area is an increasingly popular resort and features in many holiday brochures. There are shops and restaurants on the road leading to the beach and water–sports facilities on the beach itself. There is a car park on the inland side of the road and the shore is reached down some steps; it has dark coloured sand which can be painfully hot to barefooted visitors.

Also on the headland, between the bays, is the historical site of *Maa* where excavation is uncovering a late Bronze Age settlement. *Maa* seems to have had some defensive function, standing on the head-land, three sides of which are protected by steep cliffs. The remaining side was protected by a wall 11ft (3.5m) wide and with two gates. It was an ideal place for a settlement with a safe natural harbour and a nearby perennial spring although it seems to have been inhabited only sporadically and was abandoned and resettled several times, perhaps after attacks by raiders. Numerous houses have been un-covered and it could have been a miltary outpost for foreign settlers. Excavations are continuing on the site which is hard to find.

About 2 miles (3km) inland of Coral Bay, signposted from the main road, is a rough track to Mavrokolymbos dam where one can fish, if in possession of the required licence. Also in the hills is the village of **Peyia**, an attractive place which could have Byzantine origins. There are some very pretty fountains in the village square and a few tavernas spread about its winding roads.

Alternatively visitors can stay close to the coast and head out to Cape Drepanum and **Ayios Yeoryios** (Agios Georgios), on a tarred but narrow and sometimes bumpy road. Ayios Yeoryios has a few restaurants and rooms to rent along the approach road to the cape. On the headland is the site of the ruins of a sixth-century basilica. The fenced site is inland of the attractive cliff-top church and is not obvious (the sign points in the wrong direction!). The whole area was once a Roman settlement and the remains of tombs cut into the cliffs above the harbour are visible, but a good deal more excavation will be needed to uncover the true nature of the place.

The harbour is reached on a track from the headland, signed Mandoulis beach, and is very pretty with a pleasant stretch of sand. Just offshore is the island of Yeronisos, while along the coast are a number of small rocky coves.

Just outside Ayios Yeoryios is the track to **Lara**, one of the best beaches on the island and one of the hardest to reach. The best sand

---

Conservation of the Loggerhead Turtle
In 1978 a conservation project for the turtles was launched by the
fisheries department. The turtles come ashore to lay their eggs,
each one laying about 100 eggs in a hole dug in the sand and 7-8
weeks later they hatch if they have not been attacked by predators
such as foxes and crows. This conservation project is the only one
in the Mediterranean and sees about 4,000 baby turtles hatched
each year.

---

is north of the headland with its turtle hatchery; to the south the
beach is shingly. The track is appalling and the most boneshaking
trip the visitor is likely to encounter. Progress will be painfully slow
and the best beach is some 6 miles (9½km) away, but it may still be
worth persevering because it is here that some of the finest scenery
on the island can be found.

There are some interesting beaches early on the track. While they
are quiet the sea can be rough with large waves and swimmers
should take extreme care. After 5 miles (8km) on a track to the left is
a turtle hatchery. This is one of the last places in the Mediterranean
where loggerhead and greenback turtles can be found and lay their
eggs. It is also the home of the Mediterranean monk seal, another rare
species and increasing concern has been expressed by environmen-
talists that the development of this area for tourism will adversely
affect the wildlife.

Beyond the turtle hatchery are the best beaches with clear seas and
white sand. The water can suddenly become deep and there can be
a substantial surf. The long difficult drive to these beaches used to
mean they were very quiet, however these days it is possible to get
a boat from Paphos up to Lara and this means there are many more
visitors to the beach. North of Lara it becomes even more difficult to
reach the beaches and the dirt track peters out near Koppo island.

Excursions from Paphos to Ayios Neophytos

The Polis road climbs out of Paphos up to the village of **Mesoyi**
which has natural springs, used to supply Paphos with water. Here
there is a turning to **Trimithousa** and **Ayios Neophytos monastery**.

The road is at quite a high level with good views back across the
coast to Paphos. The monastery lies at the head of a wooded valley
in a pleasant setting. It is a popular place in summer as it is on the
itinerary of many of the coach tours. There are two points of interest
for visitors: the monstery itself and the caves cut out of the cliff.

Paragliding at Coral Bay

The dazzling white stone church at Peyia

Fishing in the little harbour at Ayios Yeoryios

The west coast of Cyprus towards Lara

The main part of the monastery was built in the fifteenth century but it was established in the caves in 1159 by Saint Neophytos. The saint was born in Lefkara and spent much of his early life in pilgrimage around the Middle East in search of spiritual peace. He decided to retire to a cave here but his hopes for tranquility were frustrated as news of his devotion spread and large number of followers pursued him.

He called the cave which he cut out of the rock his *enkleistra* (enclosure) and he gradually expanded it into a series of three interconnected chambers: the nave, the sanctuary and the cell. They are covered in wall paintings which were carried out under the direction of Saint Neophytos and place particular emphasis on the crucifixion and the resurrection. Also visible in the cell is the shelf where he kept his papers and his desk.

There is an interesting contrast between the primitive style of the paintings in the outer rooms to those inside which show a much more sophisticated nature, mirroring the development Byzantine art as it became subject to European influences. It is in the sanctuary (the room now containing the altar) where the paintings are best preserved. On the ceiling is a depiction of Saint Neophytos standing between the Archangels Michael and Gabriel. Above his head is the inscription, 'I fervently pray that I may be indeed enrolled among the angels by virtue of my habit'. There are numerous other paintings of the important scenes from the life of Christ.

Neophytos wrote a large number of theological treatises, including his *Ritual Ordinance* for monastic life and a history of Cyprus entitled *Concerning the Misfortunes of the Land of Cyprus*. In it he berated Richard the Lionheart saying, ' The English king, the wretch landed in Cyprus …. The wicked wretch achieved nothing against his fellow wretch Saladin but achieved this only that he sold our country to the Latines.'

The main church of the monastery is reached up some steps from the courtyard and has a domed roof over two aisles. It is dedicated to the Virgin Mary and has numerous paintings, mainly depicting the early life of Mary. In the north aisle a frieze narrates the Akaithos hymn which tells the story of the life of Christ. The saint's bones are in a wooden sarcophagus and his skull in a silver receptacle.

Paphos to Polis

Polis is 26 miles (41½km) from Paphos and although the road has been recently improved it is has some stretches with a number of bends which can make for slow progress. This is especially true in early September when the grape lorries are bringing the harvest

down from the vineyards and move at a snail's pace. Those going to
Chryssorroyiatissa monastery should allow much longer.

The early part of the journey is undramatic and beyond the turning
to Ayios Neophytos there is little settlement until **Stroumbi**, a village
which was rebuilt after an earthquake in 1953. It is a major wine and
sultana production centre and in the last week in August holds a
festival to celebrate the harvest. Ayii Anargyii has a monastic settlement which is famous for its healing water which makes it popular
with elderly people.

An alternative route to Polis, for those not in a hurry, is to turn left
here at Stroumbi. The road climbs to **Kathikas** and from here
onwards the views over the west coast are marvellous. The island of
Yeronisos off Ayios Yeoryios can be seen and further north the
beaches of Lara. In the middle ground the Avgas river starts its
dramatic drop into its gorge. The elevated road passes through the
main villages of the Laona project, a scheme to encourage tourism to
traditional village houses. After Kathikas comes **Pano Arodhes** and
Kato Arodhes, **Inia** and onto sleepy **Drousha** where the villagers
take coffee on both sides of the little square, by the white church.

Polis is now 7 miles (11km) away with views to the north over
cultivated land to Khrysokou Bay curving from Cape Arnauti to
Pomos Point in the distance. From here the road runs quickly down–
hill to Prodhromi and the outskirts of Polis.

To reach Polis quickly stay on the main route after Stroumbi and
pass through the valley on a good road. There are a number of small
villages but none of any particular interest.

Excursion to Chrissorroyiatissa Monastery

Visitors should take the main route to Polis from Paphos and turn
into the hills at Polemi, to Chryssorroyiatissa monastery. This is a
longish but worthwhile detour. The road climbs to **Tsadha** and then
Polemi once known for its topaz crystals. Like many villages in the
area it was badly damaged in the 1953 earthquake. It has a Byzantine
church with seventeenth-century icons. The road then climbs into
gentle hills which have many vineyards on their terraced slopes.
There are several villages of no great note until **Pano Panayia**, the
village where Archbishop Makarios was born. Makarios, as well as
being the leader of the church in Cyprus was its President from
Independence in 1960 to his death in 1977 and is much revered across
the island.

As a result the village has been turned into something of a shrine
to him. His parents' house, now a museum, is in the back streets a
short walk from the main road. Visitors see his parent's bed, plates

The twelfth-century wall paintings at Ayia Neophytos monastery

Passing the time of day in sleepy Drousha

A parade through the streets of Pano Panayia

Chrissorroyiatissa monastery, where the monks produce some of the best wine in Cyprus

and various photographs of him and his family. The house demonstrates very clearly the archbishop's humble origins. In the main square there is also a small museum and cultural centre which has more photographs from Makarios's presidency and various items of clothing, including items burnt in the *coup d'etat* of 1974. The building also serves as the village's cultural centre and there is a small library and photographs of recent cultural events.

A mile beyond Panayia (24miles, 38km, from Paphos) is **Chrissorroyiatissa monastery**. The name probably means the Lady of the Golden Pomegranate, although there is plenty of room for more expansive translation and the more irreverent claim a more accurate translation the 'golden breast'.

The church is impressive due to its setting at 2,000ft (610m) with fine views of the surrounding hills. It was founded by a monk called Ignatius in 1152, but the main buildings were constructed in 1770. There is an icon of the Virgin Mary set in silver and a collection of religious books. The monastery has had a turbulent history, with its buildings being burnt in 1821 by the Turks, when the priests were suspected of political agitation. More recently, during the campaign against the British, its abbot was murdered by EOKA terrorists who thought, mistakenly, that he had betrayed some of their comrades. The monastery is more peaceful these days except on 15 August when it holds a major religious festival.

The monastery is now known for its entrepreneurial skills. Its winery has been reopened and the monks produce some of the best wine in Cyprus, which is on sale in a small shop and seems very popular. They also offer the services of an icon painter who produces icons for the visitor to buy. Outside the building is a small café and a 110-year-old pine tree.

Just over a mile (1½km) away is Ayia Moni, a small church from 4AD built on top of an ancient temple to Hera. The current buildings are much later but it is in a splendid location.

From Pano Panayia some of the tracks into the mountains are passable including the road up to Kykko monstery and Throni where Makarios is buried. It should be remembered that these mountain roads are very slow and such a trip is really only for the adventurous or those with four-wheel-drive vehicles.

Visitors can descend to Polis from Chrissorroyiatissa Monastery either by the way they came or via **Simou** and **Phiti** to experience the atmosphere of the Cypriot wild west. The villages on this route are full of dilapidated whitewashed houses in a labyrinth of narrow streets. They must have the highest number of donkeys per head of any village on the island and locals look genuinely astonished at the

The Old Venetian Camel Trail

One excursion into some of the remoter parts of the island is to follow the old Venetian camel trail which passes south of Chrissorroyiatissa monastery. The trip is really only for the adventurous, with a jeep, half a day to spare and a full water bottle if travelling in summer. Drivers will also need the Government administration road map, the only one to show the trail. It must be stressed that a reliable vehicle is needed and that at the height of summer the drive will be very taxing and should only be undertaken by those with experience of such rough driving.

There are three Venetian bridges on the route: Kelephos, Elea and Roudias which is the furthest west. The bridges were built to enable their pack animals, mainly camels, to cross the river when carrying copper from the Troodos mines to Paphos. In those days the eastern river, the Dhiarizos could be a raging torrent and even today the Xeros Potamos spanned by Roudhias bridge still contains water in the dry Cypriot summer.

About 4 miles (6.5km) south of the monastery is the village of **Kilinia** and from here a stony road leads, after 2 miles (3.5km) to the eerie deserted village of **Vrecha**. The small mosque indicates that it once was a Turkish village and its inhabitants must have left after the 1974 troubles.

It is difficult to reach the remote valley which contains the trail as there are a number of different bumpy tracks. The best route is to turn right at the monument in the village centre and keeping to the right-hand fork. After about 3 miles (5km) of bad road the tree-lined river and its ruined bridge come into view. The river around Roudias bridge is a wonderful place to explore, the perennial springs form deep pools, which are ideal for swimming and idyllic in the heat of summer.

From here the camel trail runs due east and the brave visitor can follow much of the route, reaching after 10 miles (16km) the village of **Phini**. The village is known for the Pilavikou private pottery collection.

sight of a car. The roads are very bumpy and narrow, beware of donkeys coming the other way and there is a marked absence of signposts, but visitors should not panic as it seems that virtually all the roads eventually lead back to the main route.

Once back on the main tarred road **Polis** is an easy drive away. It is still a reasonably quiet place although development looks likely to occur. For the moment it is very much the haven of the backpacker and those wanting to escape the more conventional holiday trappings and as such it has a strange laid back atmosphere, found both among its visitors and the local inhabitants.

The town is built around a pedestrianised square where there are numerous restaurants, banks, a post office and some other shops. There are a few hotels in and around the town and a surfeit of rooms and apartments to rent, making it ideal for the independent traveller. There is also a campsite on the beach. Despite being a very small place, its traffic can be bad and its oneway system highly confusing. Polis is a good base for exploring the Akamas peninsula, either independently or as part of one of the organised tours advertised in the travel agents in Polis.

Near to the town, but very difficult to find, is the ancient site of *Marion*. It was founded in the seventh century BC by the Athenians and was an important centre for the export of copper. The settlement was destroyed in 312BC by Ptolemy I. A new town was then built and called *Arsinoe* after the sister of one of the Ptolemies. It was one of the ten City Kingdoms of early Cyprus. The area has been extensively excavated revealing a large number of tombs and relics, although the best finds have been put in the Cyprus Museum. There is not much left to see these days, although excavations are continuing.

West of Polis is **Lachi** (Latsi), a small fishing village with a gravelly but pleasant beach. It has a few restaurants, hotels and a bank and if any significant development is going to take place in this area it looks likely that it will occur here.

There are several good beaches in this area as one heads westwards to the *Baths of Aphrodite*, just inland from a small sandy beach. On the hill is a tourist pavilion, selling souvenirs and with its own restaurant. The Baths are in fact natural springs and a pool in the woods reached on a marked path. According to legend, Aphrodite bathed here before marrying Akamas. The setting is extremely impressive and that alone makes it worth a visit. However, try to avoid summer weekends when the babbling from the constant stream of visitors drowns out that of the spring. From the springs there is a tourist office nature trail which leads up the hill and offers splendid views of the surrounding area.

Beyond the Baths, the sweep of Khrysokou Bay up to **Cape Arnauti** is particularly impressive. This whole area, the Akamas peninsula, is one of the most beautiful on the island. It is also the home to flora and fauna which are unique in the Mediterranean, which is why the Cypriot Government has finally decided to act and is planning to make the region a national park.

There is a rough track out to the cape, suitable only for jeeps and

The unspoilt coastline of the Akamas peninsula

Lachi harbour

motorbikes. To walk there and back is nearly 12 miles (18km) and impossible and unwise in the middle of summer. It is also possible to join a guided party. Perhaps the best option is to go to the cape by boat and walk back to the Baths of Aphrodite. Boats can be hired from Lachi but it is probably wise to make arrangements to be picked up at the Baths of Aphorodite on return, either by leaving a car there or making arrangements with the boatman. The extra few miles at the end of the walk might otherwise spoil the trip.

The main attraction of the cape is billed as Fontana Amorosa, another spirng associated with Aphrodite. The area inspires eloquent descriptions in the tourist office literature but in reality is little more than a muddy goat pool. However, the surrounding countryside more than makes up for any disappointment.

Cape Arnauti, where the boat will leave visitors, is a rocky mound with no beach; there are wonderful deserted, sandy coves further east. The track back to the Baths is an easy walk, although it is very isolated and lone female visitors may feel a little uneasy. The peace is occasionally shattered by jeeps or young tourists on motorbikes. Alternatively visitors can walk closer to the shore where the scenery is even more impressive but the going a little harder. About 20 minutes walk from the cape, two rusting wrecks lie just offshore, an attraction to tourists and marine life alike.

In the distance is Polis with its splendid backcloth of hills. The middle distance is marked by the strange flat topped hill of Vakhines which can be reached up a zigzagging path on its north flank. It is about 1,000ft (300m) high and its summit is a major attraction to the really energetic — the view undisputably the best in southern Cyprus. A short distance down the main track are large red signs and flags marking the firing ranges for the British Army and clearly it is wise to stay on the marked route.

At the base of the hill the soil turns from red to white and just offshore is the little island of Ayios Yeoryios and the Baths are now only 2 miles (3km) away and the scenery still magnificent. There is a short uphill section, climbing above the sea and where the deep ruts in the track are a hazard for motorcyclists. From here it is a short walk to the tourist pavilion where the thirsty summer visitor will be able to partake of, perhaps, the best drink they have ever tasted.

East of Polis the beaches and the scenery are wonderful. The road runs close to the coast passing the headquarters of the Cyprus copper and sulphur mines to a long beach. There are a few small villages but this area is very remote and visitors will only rarely be forced to share the beach with anyone else. The road climbs up the cliffs, with some quite breathtaking views out to Pomos point and beyond with the rocky cliffside contrasting with the deep blue of the sea, a much deeper blue than on the southern side of the island. Just the other side of Pomos is a pleasant fish restaurant and harbour.

At **Pachyammos** the road turns inland to avoid **Kokkina**, a Turkish village in the Cypriot zone which is supplied by sea by the UN and therefore inaccessible to the visitor. After this extensive detour the road reaches **Pyrgos**, a small village with a beach. This is literally the end of the line, the miltary zone stops you going any further.

This is one of the least populated areas of the island and being so close to the miltary zone the tracks should only be attempted by the adventurous. There is a route back into the Troodos hills from here via Lyso and Stavros forest station but the route is tortuous and very slow. This is the habitat of the Cyprus moufflon, although it is a notoriously shy creature and it is unlikely to show itself to visitors.

Additional Information

Accommodation
Camping
Polis Campsite
☎ 06 321526
550yd (500m) from Polis town
centre, near the beach
200 places
Open: March to November

There are several hotels in Polis and some holiday firms offer accommodation in traditional houses in the area. Rooms to rent are widely advertised.

Boat Trips
From Paphos to Coral Bay and Lara
From Polis to Akamas peninsula

Places to Visit
Ayios Neophytos Monastery
Open: 7.30am-sunset

Chrysorroyiatissa Monastery
Open: all day, except siesta
(12noon-3pm)

Makarios Museum
Pano Panayia
Open: 9am-12noon, 1-5pm

Turtle Hatchery
Lara
No formal opening times, depends on the season and whether anyone or any turtles are there

Fishing
Mavrokolymbos Dam
7 miles (11km) northwest of Paphos
Ayia Marina Dam
11 miles (17km) northeast of Polis.
Pomos Dam
10 miles (16km) northeast of Polis.
Argaka Makounta Dam
7 miles (11km) northeast of Polis.

Local Events
15 August
Religious festivals at many of the monasteries

Transport
To Paphos: Amoroza Bus Co
☎ 06 321115
There are also services to the Baths of Aphrodite from Polis

Emergencies
Polis Hospital
☎ 06 321431

8

THE TROODOS MOUNTAINS

Visitors who confine themself to the coasts of Cyprus will miss out on some of the most spectacular and interesting parts of the island. The Troodos mountains, which reach heights of more than 6,000ft (1,800m), offer splendid views, extensive opportunities for walkers and in winter become a ski resort. The mountain villages too are picturesque in their own dilapidated way and there are many mountain churches with exceptionally fine wall paintings from the Byzantine period.

In summer the mountains have a major advantage over the plain below; they are cool, at least relatively speaking, and many Cypriots take advantage of this chance to escape the heat and spend their summer holidays up in the Troodos.

The Troodos region is divided into four districts: Pitsillia covering the eastern hills; the Solea valley which contains the popular hill resorts; the Marathassa valley which includes Moutoullas and Kala-panayiotis which is known for its cherries; and the Krassochoria, the wine producing area of the southern slopes.

The Troodos range was caused by the volcanic eruption which created the whole island. The mountain slopes are covered in pine trees while the valleys are fertile ground for fruit trees irrigated by the melting snows. Cyprus is known for its copper but these deposits are almost exhausted. There are rich mineral deposits of other metals, including asbestos and chrome, in the mountains.

Nicosia to Tamsassus & Machairas (Makheras)

There are few sites of interest on the route out to *Tamassus* 12 miles (19km) from Nicosia. Visitors should leave via the Strovolos suburb of Nicosia, passing the right turn to Troodos, taking the Palekhori road. Turn into Dheftera and follow the signs to Machairas and after

a short distance there are signs to *Tamassus*. This ancient site was
famous for its copper production and may have been the *Temese*
mentioned early in the Odyssey when Athene, pretending to be
Mentes, a traveller, tells Telemachus that she has been sailing in 'the
wine dark sea to a foreign land and the city of Temese; I am in quest
of copper.'

This site has been inhabited since 2,500BC and in 800BC it became
a Phoenecian colony. The mines were owned by various illustrious
monarchs ranging from Alexander the Great to Herod. It was also the
birthplace of two saints. The first was St Heraclidos, the first bishop
of Cyprus who served as guide to St Barnabas and St Paul when they

came to the island. The second was St Mnason, Heraclidos's successor who was known for performing miracles and this led to the site becoming the earliest centre of Christianity on the island.

Some ruins have been revealed in the area and a full-size statue of Apollo was found in 1836, although this was destroyed by villagers. The main items of interest to the visitor are two underground tombs, possibly of early kings but now inhabited by energetic bats.They are quite deep and reached down carved stone steps. Inside there are images cut in stone on the walls. Also on the site is a jumble of ruins of ancient houses over which the visitors can scramble, but little detail can be made out.

Just south of Tamassus village is the monastery of **Ayios Irakleidios** which originates from the Byzantine period, although most of the buildings visible today were constructed in 1759. Inside are some icons and the skull of Irakleidios, the aforementioned saint who was made a bishop by St Paul and St Barnabas, and who had a reputation for being able to heal the sick. These days the monastery is inhabited by nuns who make jam and cultivate a very pleasant garden. The whole monastery has a very tranquil aura. There is a café outside by the car park.

From here it is a pleasant drive out to **Machairas monastery**, although visitors should be aware that it is along a slow, winding road up into the mountains. The monastery is also accessible from Larnaca and Limassol, but both these trips constitute a long drive including stretches on unsurfaced roads.

The monastery is impressively sited in the pine forests and was built in 1148 by monks who claimed to have found an icon of the Virgin Mary here. The Emperor Comnenos gave them funds to build the monastery and once erected, it received many royal visitors including the wife of Hugh IV, who was allegedly struck dumb after entering the sanctuary which was forbidden to women, as it is today. The name Machairas means 'cut with a knife' which has been variously interpreted as a reference to the winter icy winds or to the icon which may have been damaged by a knife when it was found. The church contains the original icon, now covered in silver ornament, and a few other paintings

The monastery was burnt down twice — in 1530 and 1892 — and the current building shows little sign of its long history. However, it has continued to play a role in Cyprus's more recent history. Grigoris Afxentiou, the second in command of the EOKA guerillas who opposed British rule, was ambushed close to the monastery.

It is possible to continue on rough tracks further into the mountains and indeed to reach Troodos itself, but this is really only for those feeling adventurous. Alternatively one can use Machairas as a base for hill walking.

One interesting extension to the drive to Machairas is to follow the road round the monastery for 4½ miles (7km) to **Gourri**. The road is narrow and winding with a short stretch of dirt track before Lazania but is not too taxing and is a quiet, pleasant drive in the heart of the mountains. **Lazania** is a typical dilapidated mountain village tumbling down the hillside and the road skirts round it.

Just before Gourri take the road to **Fikardou**. This whole area has been declared an ancient monument with the aim of preserving the woodwork and traditional village architecture of the houses. Two houses — the house of Katsinioros and Achilleas Demetri which were built in the sixteenth century — have been restored and are open to the public. Tickets are available from the café. At the moment the village is somewhat ghostly as there are no real residents and few visitors, but as the restoration proceeds it may regain some life.

Another pleasant area to explore is that around Klirou where there are pleasant places for picnics, and easy drive from Gourri. Those coming directly from Nicosia should take the Troodos road and then head to Dheftera. From Dheftera take the right-hand fork to **Malounda** and then **Klirou**. These villages have no specific sites of interest but are attractive for being unspoiled. In spring the area is particularly pretty when the almond blossom is on the trees.

Just short of Ayios Epiphanios is a gorge, which in summer is without too much water, providing a pleasant walk along the bottom of the ravine and a rare summer opportunity to appreciate the lush vegetation on either side. From here the road heads further into the mountains and eventually to Palekhori.

Palekhori, is another pleasant village lying in wooded hills. It was owned by the Knights Templar from 1297 and then passed to the noble Venetian Ibelin family. The main sites of interest are the churches; Panayia Khrysopantanissa dates from the sixteenth century but has been extensively modernised. It has some seventeenth-century paintings, possibly by Philip Goul, a famous icon painter who travelled the Mediterranean, and a tenth-century icon of the Virgin. The village is famous for its smoked pork and sausages and is in a particularly pleasant setting, with several good restauarants.

Troodos and Mount Olympus

The main route to Troodos is found by heading west out of Nicosia and is well signposted. Once out of the suburbs of Nicosia there is a right turn at some traffic lights. The turning is well marked. Despite passing through a barren flat plain there is a surprising amount of

The monastery of Ayios Irakleidios

Lazania, a typical small village in the Troodos mountains

settlement by the road, including that built for the refugees. There are lots of roadside fruit stalls which offer the best fruit around. While most of the plain is dusty and barren, in the distance the visitor may just catch a glimpse of the sparkle of the blue sea of Morphou Bay, tantalisingly close but in the Turkish part of the island and so inaccessible.

Nineteen miles (30km) from Nicosia is **Peristerona**. It is famous for its church which lies on the west bank of the river which is virtually always dry. It has five domes arranged in the form of a cross and was built in the tenth century. There is only one other church on the island constructed in that form, that of Yeroskipos near Paphos. It contains sixteenth-century icons of the Presentation of Christ in the temple. There is also a wooden chest containing written church records and is decorated by a medieval scene painted on it.

From Peristerona there are several routes into the high mountains. The first and most usual is to continue west and then turn up to Kakopetria. Alternatively it is possible to turn south at Peristerona, heading up to Orounda and climbing up the valley reaching, eventually, the churches of Panayia tou Arakou at Lagoudhera and Stavros tou Ayiasmati. (See pages 115-17.)

West of Peristerona

Heading west of Persiterona the first site of interest is Asinou church which is reached by turning left just before Astromeritis, to Nikitari and then after a further 5 miles (8km) is **Asinou**. This is one of the most famous churches on the island and lies at 1,500ft (456m) above sea level, pleasantly situated in the hills. The paintings were restored in 1965 by a team from Harvard University. The key is available from the priest at Nikitari.

The church was probably built in 1100 by somebody called Nikepharos. This is recorded in an inscription and there is a painting which depicts him as a richly dressed bearded man. This painting is not the original but was repainted during the restoration. The church originally belonged to the monastery of Phorbiotissa, long since abandoned. There is also a picture of the donors in the narthex (vestibule) but no inscription to give any further clues as to their identity. The narthex was added in the late twelfth century and its paintings were gradually accumulated over the centuries.

The church consists of a rectangular nave covered by a barrel vaulted dome, a common design for churches of that period. It was built mainly from mud mortar which seems to have been responsible for its frequent collapses and the need for rebuilding.

There are over a hundred paintings in the church which as a whole stands as a representation of the Universe with a painting of Christ in the dome, at the centre, and below him are the Angels and Apostles. The main paintings cover all the events in the life of Christ including the Last Supper and the Crucifixion, while at the lower levels in the church are paintings of individual saints.

The church is dedicated to the Virgin Mary and there are numerous paintings depicting scenes from her life. Further details can be gained from the official guide to the church, available from the tourist office. The surrounding area is a good place for strolling in the hills or for picnics.

There are minor roads and tracks which eventually lead to Troodos but it is easier to return to **Nikitari** and take the main road towards Linou. One can either continue on the main road signed to Kakopetria or turn to **Linou** and take the more minor road from the village itself. This is also the starting point for the excursion out to Kykko monastery and the scenic route to Troodos described later.

Kakopetria and Galata are the first sites of interest where there are several important, but remarkably tiny, churches. In the middle of **Galata** is Ayia Sozomenos, with a distinctive steep pitched roof and a complete set of wall paintings. An inscription over the west door says it was built from the contributions of thirteen villagers and finished in 1513. The upper part of the walls shows the New Testament cycle. There are two paintings of the resurrection, one on the west wall and the other on the north wall. At the far end of the north wall is a striking depiction of St George spearing a green and red dragon. There are then scenes from the life of the Virgin Mary and on the lower parts of the walls pictures of individual saints.

Just below Galata is Panayia Theotokos or Archangel Michael church, off the main road. Inside the door is a painting of Christ flanked by the Virgin Mary and John the Baptist and below them the donors who were, according to the inscription, members of the Zacharia family and probably Venetian nobility. They are unusually detailed portraits of the donors. On the upper walls is the New Testament cycle and on the lower walls, as usual, the individual saints.

Pananyia Podithou stands close by and used to belong to a monastery. It was built in 1502 by the Coron family. Above the west entrance is the resurrection, in the apse scenes from the life of Moses, and a fine depiction of the Communion. In the west pediment is the Crucifixion in an extremely crowded narrative style rather than using traditional Byzantine symbolism.

Immediately south of Galata, passing yet another tiny church, is **Kakopetria**, one of the best known mountain villages on the island.

Nature Trails

There are several nature trails in the area which provide pleasant walks. A leaflet is available from the tourist office which gives details of the wildlife that might be seen on these trails. A series of numbers mark items of interest on the route which tally up with the tourist office leaflet.

The first trail is 5½ miles (9km) long and starts just outside Prodhromos, leading up to Troodos. It passes an abandoned ski lift and then onto the first of several viewing points from where most of the vineyards of the southern slopes are visible, followed by a natural spring. The walk then leads to the entrance of the chromium mine and ultimately to Troodos Square.

The second trail is 2 miles (3km) long and starts 1.2km from Troodos square, off the Olympus road. Unfortunately the tourist office signs are now beginning to fade and are very difficult to read. Keep to the narrow path, ignoring the broader routes encountered. There are seats at regular intervals and viewing points which look over the southern slopes down to Limassol. The track brings you round to the bottom of the ski slopes where the marking is less than adequate; follow the broad track to reach the main road. Turn right back down to the start.

The third trail is 3miles (4km) long and starts at Kryos Potamos, 1¼ miles (2km) from Troodos square. Turn left off the main road passing Government huts over the bridge to see the wooden arch which marks the start of the walk. Kryos Potamos is one of very few permanent streams in Cyprus. The trail follows the banks of the stream, crossing back and forth in very pleasant countryside and ends at the Kaledonia falls. There are signs listing significant plants and trees and the visitor is also likely to encounter a large number of birds. The waterfalls are fairly impressive, at least by Cyprus standards, and can also be reached by car from the trout farm just above Platres.

It is a typical Cypriot village cascading down both sides of the valley in its own distinctive ramshackle way. Its name means bad stone, apparently because of a large stone which used to lie on the hillside above the village and which was supposed to bring good luck to newly married couples. However, one unfortunate couple went to make their wish and the stone rolled over and crushed them and the stone's reputation was tarnished forever.

The village itself is a busy resort in summer for those who are trying to escape the heat of the plain and there are places to stay and many restaurants, and indeed tourist shops. It has banks and a post office and its shady cobblestoned streets are pleasant places to wander.

Three miles (5km) on a road from the village is the church of Ayios Nikolaos Tis Stegis (of the roof). In the last ½ mile the road deteriorates quite badly, making for a bumpy drive. The church is down a path from the road and has a low domed tiled roof covered by a huge steep pitched one. It was built in the eleventh century with later additions. It lies by a stream which, unusually for Cyprus, never dries up and visitors will hear the sound of running water.

The church has a complete set of paintings covering the New Testament cycle. Of particular note is the raising of Lazarus and Transfiguration in the west vault, which is particularly expressive, as is the Triumphant entry of Christ into Jerusalem. The Forty Martyrs are also very impressive and much copied on postcards; they were betrayed by one of their comrades and put to death for their Christian beliefs. The paintings show several different styles and in the lower parts of the nave are life-size depictions of saints.

Beyond Kakopetria the road begins to climb steeply and a real sense of the height of these mountains is gained as your ears begin to pop. There are several rather dilapidated cafés by the side of the road and a pleasant picnic site at **Platanias**. On the side of the mountain is the grey scar of the Amiandos Mine. It extracts asbestos with seemingly little concern for the effect on the environment of its activities except perhaps for the sanatorium, curiously juxtaposed next to it.

Troodos village is next, not really a village but a collection of shops, cafés and hotels which becomes chaotic in the winter skiing season and when the tourist buses come up in summer. Despite appearances the cafés offer some of the best kebab on the island.

From here it is a short drive to Mount Olympus, at 6,404ft (1,946m) the highest peak on the island and from where there are spectacular views of the surrounding area. On a clear day the keen eyed might see Turkey. The summit itself is well known for the white 'golf balls' which are the outward sign of the military listening post.

The Eastern Hills

The eastern Troodos are bare and covered in scrub, unlike the pine clad hills further west, although the lower slopes have been terrraced to provide room to grow vines.

An interesting, although taxing, excursion is to the churches of Stavros tou Ayiasmati and Panayia tou Arakou at Lagoudhera which contain some of the finest Byzantine church wall paintings on the island. The drive should not be attempted late in the day as the roads are narrow and winding and the priest is less likely to be available to unlock the churches. Visitors should note that both churches have now been surrounded by protective walls and roof so that little impression of them can be gained from the exterior.

The route leaves Troodos via **Kyperounda** then leads into the rather dilapidated village of **Khandria** where the road starts to degenerate. A good 25 minutes drive away is the village of **Laghoudera**, but be careful not to end up on the road to Polystipos. At the far side of the village is the church of Panayia tou Arakou. Ask at the café for the key and the priest will show you round.

It was Byzantine in origin, but parts of it have since been rebuilt. It is a single-aisled vaulted building with a steep pitched roof and contains one of the most complete collections of paintings of the Byzantine period, which have been restored very well. Over the north door is the dedication stating the church was donated in 1192 by Lord Leon, son of Authentis, who was a Byzantine noble or

The village of Khandria in the central Troodos

governor of the region.

There is some dispute over the meaning of the name of the church. Some say it is from *Arakas* (pea) in the tradition of using vegetable symbols for the Virgin Mary, others, more romantically, claim it is derived from *Hierax* (hawk) because a hawk pointed out where the icon of the Virgin could be found.

In the dome is the painting of Christ the Pantokrator (ruler of the universe), looking serene and surrounded by angels and then by a choir of twelve prophets. These are followed by depictions of the Annunciation, with the Archangel Gabriel approaching Mary who is calmly sewing. In the northern recess is a very striking picture of the Virgin Mary being presented at the temple. This is followed by a complete depiction of the nativity which is very well painted. Then comes the presentation to the temple of the child Christ, who is wearing a silver earring in his left ear. This scene is highly original and breaks the traditions normally observed for the scenes, by replacing Anna with John the Baptist.

In the northwest recess is the baptism of Christ by St John. The crucifixion is missing from the sequences on the west wall, probably lost when the church was extended. The next painting is the Anastasis (Christ's descent to Hades), followed by the ascent to Heaven and the Dormition of the Virgin Mary. Other pictures include that of the Archangel Michael on the south wall and a wide variety of different saints which complete an extremely fine collection of Byzantine art.

The key for the church of Stavros tou Ayiasmati can be obtained in **Platanistasa**, a pretty hill village with a medieval church of its own. The priest will not go to the church late in the day as there is no electricity making it impossible to see the paintings once the light fades. Stavros tou Ayiasmati lies on an isolated hillside northwest of the village, 2½ miles (4km) down a dirt track off the main road.

It has the typical steep pitched roof and the inscription over the door states it was founded by Peter Peratis and his picture is on the south wall. The walls of the nave are divided into two zones. The upper one shows festivals and narrative paintings, while the lower levels focus on individual saints. There are thirty compositions in the New Testament cycle, starting with the birth of the Virgin Mary and passing through the Annunciation to the crucifixion. That showing the nativity is distinctive due to the crowded nature of the scene, every possible character is depicted in it. The Betrayal scene is particularly colourful and dramatic while the Last Supper has all the disciples with their initials above their heads. The Crucifixion is a simpler scene and the cycle ends with the depiction of the death of

---

Skiing in the Troodos Mountains

In winter Troodos turns itself into a ski resort. The first snow usually falls in late December and lasts until the end of March. There is a ski shop where equipment can be hired and tickets for the lifts are on sale. There are two skiing areas with a total of four ski lifts. The first is Sun Valley which is for beginners and has a run of 166yd (150m) from the top of the ski lift. On the same hill is a longer more testing route called Sun Valley 2 which has its own lift. Both slopes are busy at weekends.

The North Face is the other skiing area which offers steep descents of up to 1,148ft (350m). Sometimes competitions are held on these slopes. The roads are usually kept open by snow plough but at times drivers will need chains to get through. While it is often sunny visitors should remember that these mountains are very high and should ensure they have warm clothing.

---

the Virgin Mary.

In the north recess are ten miniatures showing historical scenes. These are a very rare departure from the usual strictly religious paintings of this period and show the former glories of the Byzantine Empire, including Constantine's battle for Rome in 312, as well as scenes from the Old Testament. There are also numerous pictures of saints, including St John the Baptist and St George on a white charger which can be found to the the right of the doorway.

The paintings have been restored under the auspices of UNESCO and the priest knows enough English to explain them, but any conversation apart from this is impossible. While admission is free the priest expects visitors to buy souvenirs.

This area is also accessible from Limassol, taking the road up to **Louvaras** where there is another Byzantine church, **Zoopyi**, and then **Agros**. The narrow mountain road makes this slow going.

The Southern Hills

There are several places of interest in the southern hills of Troodos. The first, heading down from Troodos, is the **Troodhitissa monastery**. It was probably founded in 1250 as a shrine for an icon of the Virgin which may have been hidden here originally in a cave in the eighth century. Just short of the monastery beyond the waterfall is a pathway up to a small cave where a copy of the icon can still be seen. The current church dates from 1731. It contains numerous icons including the original one, now plated with silver.

Down the road is **Platres**, the largest mountain resort, which has several hotels and restaurants. It is extremely popular in summer with locals from the plains. It is distinctive for having a perennial stream flowing through it, giving the village an unusually verdant quality. There are buses from Limassol and Nicosia. The village is divided in two, Kato (lower) and Pano (upper) Platres. Kato Platres is quiet and not overrun by tourists. In the upper part, in the main square, is a tourist office, bank and post office. There are also several hotels and restaurants. The Kaledonian Falls are just upstream, accessible on foot or by car from the trout farm at the top of the village.

The road from Platres then descends the 26 miles(41½km) back to Limassol. The hills are quite gentle and the drive quite easy. It passes through various wine producing areas and there are fruit stalls outside virtully every house selling whatever is in season, as well as honey from mountain bees. **Trimiklini**, the largest place on the route, is a pretty village with a few restaurants. From here it is a very quick trip to Limassol.

Pedhoulas, dominated by its modern church

Kykko monastery

The modern frescoes at Kykko monastery

Archboshop Makarios

Makarios was born in Panayia on 13 August 1913 and in 1926 joined the Kykko monastery as a novice. He then studied in Athens and was ordained in 1946, becoming Bishop of Kition in 1948 and soon after Archbishop. He then formed the focus of the demands for independence. After abortive negotiations in 1955 he was exiled to the Seychelles by the British but he took part in the subsequent conferences which finally led to agreement on independence. After independence he became President, embodying the link that had always existed between political action and the Church. The coup of 1974 attempted to depose him but he escaped and returned some months later after the island had been divided by the Turkish invasion. He died of a heart attack in 1977, but remains a potent figure for Greek Cypriots, both in the religious and political sphere.

Scenic Route to Troodos and Kykko

This route up to Troodos from Nicosia has the best views on the island, passing through many traditional mountain villages. The road passes close to the village of Linou and then after 6 miles (9½km) turns up into the hills on a winding route characterised by tight hairpin bends and fine views. The first village of interest is that of **Kalopanayiotis**, which has a dam close by and a sulphur spring. Just below the village and well signposted is the monastery of **Ayios Ioannis Lampadistis** which has an eleventh-century church; a later Latin chapel and numerous additions from other periods, and this mixture of styles is particularly interesting. It also has some fine frescos from the thirteenth and fifteenth centuries. The paintings in the church are currently being restored. A major religious festival is held here on 4 October every year.

The next village is that of **Moutoullas**, which is famous for its spring water which is bottled and sold around the island. Then comes **Pedhoulas** which is extremely beautiful when the cherry blossom is out in the surrounding orchards and there are always fruit stalls by the side of the road selling local produce. It has a small church, built in 1474, with a limited series of paintings from the new Testament. There are several shops and hotels and it is dominated by the modern, silver-domed Archangelos Michael church. The steep paths of the village are very pleasant to wander along.

Prodhromos, at a height of 4,560ft (1,368m), is the highest village on the island and it has several hotels as it is a popular summer

retreat. This means at weekends it can be very busy, and is best used
as a base for exploring the surrounding area. From here the road
climbs up to Troodos, passing Prodromos Dam where there is a
picnic site and forestry department trails. As the road makes its final
ascent the views are stunning especially in the early morning when
the mist is rising off the mountains and the coast begins to shimmer
below.

A worthwhile trip is to **Kykko monastery**, 15 miles (24km) from
Pedhoulas. It is the best known of Cyprus's monasteries and the most
significant for the Greek Orthodox church. The road leaves from
Pedhoulas, passing the huge cross on the hill and then on through
uninhabited mountains. Drivers should, however, beware of the
large tourist buses thundering up and down. The monastery lies at
a height of 3,816ft (1,160m) which means it is often cool even in the
height of summer and in winter can be bitterly cold.

It was founded in the twelfth century being given to Isaiah, a
hermit who had cured the Emperor Alexios Comnenos' daughter of
sciatica. The monastery received an icon of the Virgin Mary which,
it is claimed, was painted by St Luke. These days the icon is the main
attraction of the monastery. As it is considered too sacred to look at
it has to be covered by a silver plate on which is embossed a
representation of the icon itself. The building suffered damage in
four fires in 1356, 1542, 1751 and 1813, but the icon always survived.

It is the biggest and richest monastery on the island and in its
treasury is a rich collection of bishop's crowns, an early Bible and
other relics. It has frequently been a sanctuary for political activists
and in 1956 was a mountain hideout for General Grivas, the leader
of EOKA, the terrorist group which fought for independence from
the British.

The monastery has strict dress rules and those deemed to be
immodestly dressed will be issued with striped bathrobes which do
little for their dignity. Visitors can wander round most of the monastery, there are modern mosaics and paintings on the walls of all the
cloisters and in the church where the pious take the opportunity to
kiss the icon. There is a small museum containing religious artefacts,
including old Bibles and surplices.

A festival is held here every year during 14-16 August when it is
overrun with locals. In fact the monastery is always busy and the
attempts made to preserve its tranquility seem to be in vain with
great queues of visitors noisily escorted by their guides seemingly
ever present. Below the monastery is a tourist pavilion, a new
complex of rooms and stalls selling traditional Cypriot sweets.

A little further up the road behind the monastery is the burial site of Archbishop Makarios at **Throni,** which has now become a sort of shrine. The trees around are all bedecked with fragments of clothing as a homage to the dead Archbishop. His tomb is guarded by two extremely bored-looking soldiers. A short distance up the hill is Throni itself where a famous icon of the Virgin can be seen. From the path around the hill there are some wonderful views of the surrounding area.

From here it is possible to head further into the hills on non metalled roads, which are slow but passable. Ultimately one reaches the forest station at **Stavros tis Psokas**, where there is a café and a hostel where it is sometimes possible to stay. There is another more southerly route which passes through **Cedar Valley** — an area with the peaceful and unspoilt atmosphere of the high mountains and it is an ideal area for those who want to get away from from it all.

Life still follows its traditional way in the foothills of the Troodos

Additional Information

Accomodation
Camping
Troodos Campsite
2km (1½ miles) from Troodos
square on the Troodos to
Kakopetria road.
☎ 05 421624

Youth Hostel
Troodos
400m from the square
Open: July-Aug 7.30-10am, 4pm-
10pm

Other Accommodation
Stavros tis Psokas
Beds are available at the forest
station. These should be booked in
advance.
☎ 06 722338

Accommodation is also available in
monasteries. Some do not admit
women.

There are many hotels in Platres,
Pedhoulas and Kakopetria, ranging
from the grandeur of the Churchill
to more modest establishments.

Places to Visit
Tamassos Archaeological Site
Off Machairas road
Open: May-Sept Tues-Sat 9am-12
noon, 4-7pm; Oct-Apr Tues-Sun
9am-1pm, 2-4.30pm

*House of Katsinioros and Achilleas
    Dimitri*
Fikardou village
(tickets from the café)
Open: May-Sept Wed-Sun 10am-
1pm, 4-6pm, Oct-Apr 10am-1pm,
3pm- 5pm

Churches can be visited all day
except at siesta time. However,
many churches are kept locked and
it will be necessary to ask in the
nearest village for the key. The
following are of special note:

Asinou Church
Beyond Nikitari
Key from priest in Nikitari.

Ayios Iraklidios Monastery
South of Politiko village

Ayios Nikolaos tis Stegis
Open: 10.30am-4pm

Kykko Monastery
Open all day except at siesta time

Machairas Monastery
Open all day except at siesta time

Peristerona Church
Key from the café next door

Panayia tou Arakou
Laghoudera
Ask in the village for the key.

Church of Stavros tou Ayiasmati
3 miles (5km) beyond Platanistasa
Key available in the village

Troodhitissa Monastery
Between Platres and Prodhromos
Open all day except at siesta

Fishing
Angling in dams is only permitted
with a licence and the dams are
only open at certain times of the
year. Licences are available from
the district fisheries departments in
Nicosia, Limassol, Larnaca or Paphos.

Prodromos Dam
Between Troodos and Prodromos
Kalopanayiotis Dam

Local Events

In the mountain villages there are numerous celebrations of the saint's days.

The monasteries also celebrate the saints to which they are dedicated. Between 14 and 16 August there are grand celebrations and pilgrimages to the churches dedicated to the Virgin Mary.

August
Omodhos Wine Festival

Animal Sanctuary

There is a sanctuary for the Cyprus moufflon in the Paphos forest near Stavros forest station.

Sports

Skiing
Cyprus Ski Club
PO Box 2185
Nicosia
☎ 02 365340

Walking
There are opportunities for walking in most areas, although walkers will have to create their own routes. In May-Sept strenuous walking is to be avoided and even those on shorter walks should ensure they have a plentiful supply of water. In winter there are all the usual hazards of high mountains including snow and fog and visitors need to take as much care as in more northern climates. Detailed maps, 1:50,0000 (series K717), published by the UK Ministry of Defence may be available to official users. Contact the Department of Lands and Surveys in Niosia.

Horse Riding
There are opportunities for horse riding from Troodos Square or arranged through the larger hotels.

Tourist Offices

Platres (in main square)
☎ 05 421316
Open May-Sept only

Transport
There are bus services to the hill resorts from Limassol and Nicosia but these tend to run only once a day.

Emergencies
☎ 199 for police, fire and ambulance.

9

NICOSIA

Nicosia is the capital of the island and lies in the Central Plain, the Mesaoria. Its inland setting helped to protect it from the Arab raiders who devastated so many of the coastal towns. As a result much of its history is still visible today, standing side by side with the modern, busy city.

The origins of Nicosia are unclear, although it may be on the site of the ancient settlement of *Ledra* but no significant archaeological remains have been found to confirm that view. The first indications that it was a settlement of any importance come in the fourth century BC when it was probably rebuilt and enlarged by Lefkos the son of Ptolemy; hence the origin of its Greek name, *Lefkosia*.

It was not until the seventh century, when the coastal towns were being ravaged by pirate raids, that Nicosia came into its own and its prosperity grew during the Lusignan period when the royal court was set up here and many public buildings were constructed. Despite the general affluence, the city suffered from several natural disasters in this period, including frequent earthquakes and outbreaks of plague.

Manmade disasters also occurred, for instance when the Mamelukes crossed the island to make a raid on the city in 1426 which was successful, despite the extensive defences which had been erected. For the next sixty years the town was ruled, indirectly, from Egypt. However, the Venetians took control in 1489 and built up the city walls which are a central part of the character of the city. Despite their massive construction the walls proved of little use when the Turks made their attack. The city fell after only six weeks, in a real bloodbath in which 20,000 people died.

Under the Turks the city declined and in 1764 riots led to the death of the Turkish governor. The bloody history continued and in 1821

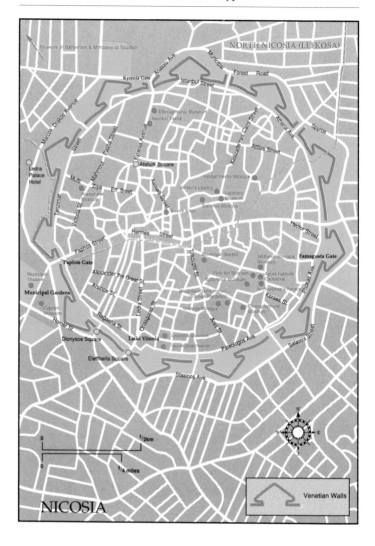

NICOSIA

Venetian Walls

200 Christians were killed by a particularly ferocious governor, Kuchuk Mehmed.

The town was the seat of the British Governor from 1878 and many of the administrative buildings date from that colonial period. The city had long had a Greek and Turkish sector and in the wake of the

Statue of Archbishop Makarios outside the Archbishop's Palace, Nicosia

A traditional barber's shop in Old Nicosia

independence settlement proved one of the key places where the tension between the two communities led to violence. In 1964 fighting broke out between Greeks and Turks and the city was informally divided by the UN. Then in 1974 when Archbishop Makarios was overthrown in the military coup, the Turks invaded and the city was divided along the green line. This means that Greeks and Turks cannot pass from one side of the city to the other, although tourists can get permission to cross from the south to the north for a day through the Ledra Palace checkpoint (see Fact File).

South Nicosia

There are plenty of hotels in the southern part of the city, ranging from the luxurious to the spartan. A wide range of restaurants are available offering cuisine from many countries. Nicosia is a very busy city and with the traffic whirling round parking can be difficult. If possible avoid the evening rush hour between 5pm and 7pm when the cacophony of hooting can distract even the most experienced of drivers. There are several large car parks in the moat of the city walls near Eleftheria Square.

Eleftheria Square stands at the main thoroughfare between the old and the new town and is a good place for visitors to get their bearings. On the east side of the square is the D'Avila bastion which now houses the post office, municipal library and the town hall. The square itself crosses the moat and is a busy place lined with the typically Cypriot newspaper kiosks.

The tourist office is in Laiki Yitonia at the head of Onasgoras Street which runs parallel to it. Laiki Yitonia, which means local neighbour-hood, is an area of the town which has been restored and pedestrian-ised. It houses many handicraft and souvenir shops and some pleasant traditional restaurants and it is a very pleasant place to wander. It is now planned to extend the idea to other parts of the city.

 On Hyppocratous Street, also in the Laiki Yitonia area, in a restored nineteenth century building is the **Leventis Museum**, the most modern and sophisticated museum on the island. It charts the history of Nicosia right up to the present day and is named after is benefactor, Anastasios Leventis, whose foundation supports many cultural projects across the island.

The medieval findings are in the basement. Upstairs on the first floor are items from 2,300BC to the Turkish period. Among the exhibits are mannequins in Venetian costume and early books about Cyprus. The ground floor has perhaps the most interesting artefacts. They focus on the colonial history and the impact of British rule on Cyprus is very clear. Finally there is a video outlining the city's recent history and its division in 1974. There is a small museum shop in the foyer and a coffee shop in the basement.

Hyppocratous Street leads out into Onasagoras Street. This, along with Ledra street which runs parallel to it, is the main shopping street of the old city. These streets are narrow, filled with impatient traffic and dark, tiny shops. The best policy is to take one of the streets to the road block at the far end which divides the city and then turn back up the other. Visitors should take care as the pavements are very narrow and the traffic moves very fast.

There is an abundance of shops selling textiles with their rolls of cloth further blocking the pavement. This is also the place to buy jewellery. The main shops are not specifically aimed at tourists but offer a wide range of clothes, toys, indeed almost anything you would expect to find at home. There are also several good ice cream shops.

From the top of Ledra Street one can head west along the walls to reach Dionysos Square — another busy, bustling area which contains the main bus station. Head down Homer Street and then turn right into the broad Museum Avenue to reach the **Cyprus Museum** which was established in 1883 and contains many of the best archaeological finds from across the island.

Taking an anti-clockwise direction round the museum, Room 1 contains Neolithic artefacts from around the island. There are a large number of Steatite idols and on the right-hand side as you enter is the wall painting found at *Kalavassos*. It shows a headless man with his hands up. Room 2 covers the bronze age with many vases and jugs decorated with rather endearing animals. The clay figurines in the centre case are interesting in depicting worshippers at an altar.

Room 3 has exhibits of Mycenenan artefacts from *Kourion* including some fine decorated jugs and some pottery from the Hellenistic and Roman periods. The decoration is quite sophisticated and the pottery in the centre case is particularly delicate. Room 4 includes the real highlight of the museum: votive figures from 7-6BC, found at *Ayia Irini* near Morphou. The figurines are displayed as they were found, gathered around a single altar. They include minotaurs, warriors and charioteers of different sizes. Out of 2,000 figurines only two were female.

Rooms 5 and 6 serve as a sculpture gallery with artefacts from a wide range of periods. The bearded man on the left-hand side from Tamassus is particularly impressive. Room 7 contains a limestone female statue from *Soli* and a huge bronze statue of the Emperor Septimus Severus. Room 8 has bronze tools and assorted weaponry as well as some statues of gods. The tiny stone seals are very

---

Walking Tours of South Nicosia

The tourist office runs two organised walking tours. The first on Thursday morning explores the main sites of the old city. Perhaps more interesting though, is that on Monday mornings which explores the Kaimakli suburb. Visitors travel in a traditional Cyprus bus. Kaimakli is known for its stone masons and wood carvers as well as for its milk and cheese. Apparently, its name comes from the Greek word which means the froth on the top of the milk. The buildings of the area date from the eighteenth and nineteenth centuries often with mock Ionic columns. The tour also includes a stop at a coffee shop. Visitors should contact the tourist office in Laiki Yitonia for more details.

---

interesting as are the Egyptian amulets and the green-horned god from *Engomi*.

Room 11 is up some stairs and contains a mosaic showing a dog and partridge. There are also some very impressive items from *Salamis* including a huge bronze cauldron, an ivory chair, bed and throne. Room 12 has temporary exhibitions. At the time of writing this is an exhibition of ancient metallurgy.

Room 9 is underground and has representations of rock-cut tombs (2,500BC-400BC) along with the objects found in them. Room 10 has votive inscriptions and other artefacts from tombs, while Room 13 has marble statues from *Salamis*. Room 14 contains terracotta figurines and leads back to the entrance. There are statues in the garden.

Just beyond the museum on the opposite side of the road are the municipal gardens. These are full of trees and flowers and provide a welcome relief from the rush of the city. There are two small aviaries, one near the entrance and one near the children's playground containing larger birds, including vultures. Also in the gardens is the municipal theatre which has regular productions of Greek and international plays and is home to the state subsidised theatre. Over the road is the British Council which stages plays and has a fine English language library.

At the end of the main road, beyond the roundabout is the green line. Visitors can re-enter the old city through the **Paphos Gate**. This is a rather strange experience as, for a hundred yards or so, traffic enters the UN buffer zone under the scrutiny of UN soldiers from their watchtower. Entry is perfectly legitimate and the gate is still one of the main thoroughfares into the old city, though it is a stark reminder of the division of the city.

Gardens alongside the Venetian walls, Nicosia
Archangelos Gabriel monastery, Nicosia

There are also several sites of interest in the eastern side of the old city. The **Omerye mosque** lies down Trikoupis street about ½ mile from the walls, turn into the old city at Canning Bridge. As with so many mosques it was once a church, originally built in the fourteenth century and then when the Turks took over was converted in 1577 by Mustapha Pasha. He thought that the prophet Omer had stayed here and therefore merited some commemoration. On the floor are Lusignan tombstones, used by the Turks to refloor the building. The minaret is particularly tall and dominates this part of the city. It is still used as a mosque by visiting Moslems. Opposite the mosque are the domes of a Turkish Bath which is still in use today.

A short distance east of the mosque on Patriarchou Grigoriou Street is Hadjigeorjakis House (Kornak mansion). It is a fine example of Turkish architecture with a closed balcony and impressive wood-work. Hadjigeorjakis was the great Dragoman of Cyprus during 1779-1809, the official interpreter of the island, a highly prestigious position. He later left for Constantinople and was arrested and executed in 1809. The house has now been restored and houses the **Ethnographical Museum**. In the garden are fragments of tomb-stones, arches and the torsos of statues. The museum is upstairs. One enters through a reconstruction of the original living room. Going in an anti-clockwise direction, in the first room are documents from Hadjigeorjakis's life, mainly his letters to various governors and consuls. The second room gives a history of the house and its restoration. There are then various paintings and family heirlooms, including weapons. Pictures of the last two members of the family are on the wall of a subsequent room. The remaining rooms are reconstructions of a study and a bedroom.

Heading north on Zenon of Kition Street one reaches the **Arch-bishop's Palace**, a grandiose building which is meant to look Venetian in style. It was actually built in 1957 and has Archbishop Makarios' bedroom preserved along with his heart which is kept in a special case. It can only be visited on special occasions. Outside is a bust of Archbishop Kyprianos who was hanged by the Turks in 1821. There is also a huge black brooding statue of Archbishop Makarios.

A foundation for cultural projects was set up in the memory of Archbishop Makarios and as part of this the **Byzantine Museum** was established in the arcaded rooms of the old archbishopric in the same square as the palace. It contains icons from the eight to the eighteenth centuries, alongside an art gallery with more modern paintings. There is also a cultural centre and plans for further development under the auspices of the foundation. Another establishment within the old Archbishopric is the **Folk Art Museum** which was opened in 1962. The exhibits include a watermill, weaving looms, chests and hand-woven costumes.

The **Ayios Ioannis cathedral** stands next to the palace and in centre of the courtyard. It was once a Benedictine monastery where it is claimed that the finger of John the Baptist was preserved until the Mamelukes stole it. It then became a Greek Orthodox monastery and the present buildings were constructed in 1660. It contains eight-eenth-century paintings, including that of the Last Judgment and a depiction of the discovery of the bones of St Barnabas.

The **National Struggle Museum** just north of the Archbishopric has documents and photographs from the 1955-9 period, when Cyprus was fighting for independence from Britain, and exhibits from the 1974 troubles. The museum's propagandist stance may not be to the taste of some visitors.

About five minutes' walk away, keep heading north, is the **Taht el Fal mosque** in a pleasant area which is being restored. The houses are all freshly painted and there are stone benches in the pedestrianised area. The area will ulitmately resemble Laiki Yitonia.

Famagusta Gate, once known as Porto Giuliana, lies east of here at the end of Ammochostos street. It is the best preserved of the old city gates and was always the most important entrance to the city. There is a long passage cut through the gate into the moat and on both sides are guardrooms. It is decorated with numerous coats of arms, and is now a cultural centre where exhibitions are held. Also in the area are a number of new art galleries and a theatre which puts on *avant garde* productions.

Perhaps the most impressive sights in the city are the **Venetian walls** themselves which, although they are crumbling in parts, are still spectacular, being 2 miles (3km) in circumference. There were walls around the city from a very early period. The Venetians built the current inner walls with their eleven bastions and three fortified gates: Famagusta, Kyrenia, and Paphos. From Famagusta Gate you can walk back to the main city along or close to the walls passing a huge statue of various bronze figures, known as the statue of liberty. In the moat there are several pleasant parks and gardens, the best being behind Famagusta gate which contains several sculptures.

THE NEW TOWN
The new town is full of wide modern streets. Archbishop Makarios Avenue is the focus of the area, lined with shops and pavement cafés as well as new shopping malls which seem to be springing up all along the road. The Presidential Palace is to the south of the new

town on Presidential Palace Street. It was built by the British but was burnt down in 1931. It was rebuilt and used as the official presidential residence after independence, only to be burnt down again in the coup in 1974. It has been rebuilt again, but is closed to the public.

The suburbs of the town are mainly residential but are interesting to drive through quickly or to stroll in the evening and watch the Cypriots out on their balconies enjoying the cooler hours. One place of interest is the **Kykko Metochi**, a dependency of Kykko monastery in the heart of the Strovolos suburbs, at the junction of Grivas Dighenis Avenue and Ayios Prokopios Street. It is possible to wander around the cloisters and look at the painted church. The buildings, while not old, are an interesting and typical example of Cypriot religious architecture.

North Nicosia [*Lefkosa*]

Nicosia is a divided city: the southern half occupied by Greek Cypriots the northern half by Turkish Cypriots. The main entrance for those staying in the north of the island is Kyrenia Gate, although there are several other points of access. Those in the south will have to cross at the military checkpoint at the old Ledra Palace Hotel and will only be allowed across for the day. At the time of writing visitors have to return by 5.30pm and cannot enter the north after 2pm. These regulations may change and there have been periods where the border has been closed completely.

Passport numbers are taken on the Greek side and then visitors have the eerie experience of walking through no man's land overlooked by the Ledra Palace Hotel which now serves as barracks to the UN soldiers. At the Turkish checkpoint there is various form filling to be executed and a nominal charge of CY£1. Posters and signs bombard the visitor with propaganda from both sides.

Northern Nicosia has long had a Turkish sector, with a different atmosphere to the Greek part and this is even clearer today with the military division of the city. There is a strong military presence, although many of the soldiers are simply local boys doing their military service and who seem to spend more of their time shopping than on guard.

The buildings of northern Nicosia seem a little dilapidated, and were neglected during the uncertain times after the 1974 war. Development was constrained by difficult economic conditions but these days prosperity seems to be returning. In any case, this faint air of decay is part of the charm of the place which the visitor will sense as they enter a narrow maze of streets and tiny dark shops. It is easy to get lost, but as the old city covers such a small area visitors will

Kyrenia [Girne] Gate,
North Nicosia

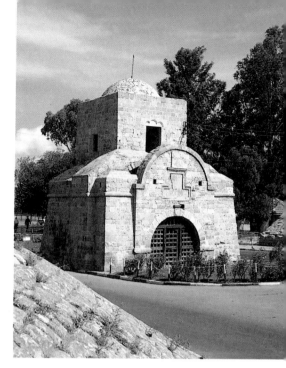

Kurmarcilar Khan,
North Nicosia

eventually emerge back onto a main road. While the local population are friendly, very few speak English.

✳ **Kyrenia [*Girne*] Gate** is one of the three gateways to the city through the Venetian walls. It was also known as Porta del Proveditore after Proveditore, a Venetian military architect. It was extended by the Turks in 1821 and above the arched entrance are verses from the Koran. The British built a new entrance so the old gate now stands rather incongruously in the middle of the road. The park across the road has a café and is where most of the buses leave for other parts of the island.

▯ Heading into the old city down Girne Caddesi, the first site of interest is the **Mevlevi Tekke**, on the left-hand side of the road. This was the home of the dervishes who were famous for their whirling dances. The dance was performed by sixteen dervishes dressed in black and white gowns and tall hats. It would start with the chant of a singer and pipe music at which point the dervishes would begin to rise and spin with arms outstretched, right palm down, left palm up.

▣ The Tekke was built in the seventeenth century and is now a museum for Turkish art and handicrafts. Exhibits include a statue and a painting of a dervish as well as musical instruments, costumes, including a fine collection of wedding dresses and embroidery. From the musician's gallery the visitor looks down on the stage upon which the dervishes whirled. Next to the mosque is a mausoleum with a long line of tombs of the sheikhs of the city.

Further up the road, in the centre of town is Attaturk Square, the main square of the city where the post office, travel agents serving as a tourist office and the city's main hotel can be found. By a round-
✳ about is a Venetian column brought in from *Salamis* in the fifteenth century to form part of a mosque. It used to carry a sculptured lion and when this was lost, it was replaced by a copper dome. The coats of arms of Venetian nobles are visible on the column. There is also a fountain from the Ottoman period, in the square.

▯ West of the square is the **Arabahmet mosque** which was built in the seventeenth century and restored in 1845. It was built to comemmorate Arab Ahmet Pasha, a Turkish conqueror of Cyprus. It has a large hemispherical dome with three smaller ones covering the porch. It is claimed that it contains part of the Prophet's beard and one hair can be shown to the believers. It is a fine building, with a fountain and the tombs of two Turkish governors in the courtyard along with that of Kamil Pasha, who rose from relatively humble origins to become Grand Vizier of the Ottoman Empire.

Beyond Arabahmet is Dervish Pasha Konagi which was built in 1807. Dervish Pasha was the editor of the first Turkish newspaper on the island and this is his two storey house which was restored in 1988 to make the **Ethnographic Musem**. One of the floors has reconstructions of a bedroom, dining room, bride's room and a weaving room. These are all set around a courtyard which has many flowers and trees.

Turning left from Attaturk square is the **Buyuk Haman** which was once a Christian church, that of St George of the Latins. It was built in the fourteenth century and then converted into Turkish baths which are still used as such today. The friendly owner will show you round either as a sightseer or a bather. There is a fountain in the centre room which leads into the cold room and then the hot room which is incredibly humid and gives clarity to the expression 'hot as a Turkish Bath'.

Nearby is the **Kumarcilar Khan** once an inn with fifty-two rooms on two floors, built around a courtyard. There are now shops and cafés built into its walls. Ask at the café to go into the courtyard.

A much more important monument is **Buyuk Khan**, another inn which was built in 1572. It had sixty-eight rooms on two storeys with an octagonal mosque in the central courtyard. Its walls have the look of battlements and it once served as a prison. The building now overlooks a car park and currently is not officially open to the public as it is being restored.

Just south of here is a pedestrianised area with many shops and a lively atmosphere. The goods on sale range from carpets to jewellery and tend to spill out onto the pavement to join the market traders selling fruit from barrows.

At the far end of Arasta Street is the **Selimiye mosque**, one of the most impressive medieval buildings in Nicosia. Its twin minarets dominate the whole city and serve as a useful landmark. It was originally built as the Latin Santa Sophia cathedral. These days it looks a little dilapidated, although its former grandeur can still be appreciated. Construction started in 1209, and the building was consecrated in 1326, although even then it was still unfinished.

There is a strong French influence visible in the design of the porch and the windows of the cathedral. It has high vaulted arches supported on massive pillars and used to be the place where the Lusignan kings were crowned. The Genoese and the Mameluke invasion damaged the building and on the Turkish arrival in 1570 it was converted into a mosque and the twin minarets added. It is still used for Muslim services and prayers but visitors may go inside if suitably dressed. One enters through the Gothic nave where there is a small chapel in which the Lusignan princes were crowned.

On the southern side of the mosque is another fourteenth-century

Gothic church. When the Turks took over in 1570 it was turned into a grain store. It is now known as Bedesten which means 'covered market'. Its north door is still impressive and carries six Venetian coats of arms, while inside are some medieval tombstones. It is not, however, open to the public. The new market lies opposite the Bedesten.

Directly behind the mosque are two smaller buildings. The first is the chapter house which was a meeting place for priests in the medieval period and is now used by the Office of Antiquities. The second building is the **Sultan's library** built in 1829. It has a good collection of oriental books, including decorated copies of the *Koran*. Inside is an inscription in praise of Sultan Mahmut II. If it is closed permission to visit can be gained from the Kumarcilar Kahn office.

To the northeast of the Selimiye mosque is the Latin **Archbishopric Palace**. Originally built in the fourteenth century, it was taken over and extended by the Turkish governors. It contains some interesting wood carvings.

A short walk away is the **Lapidary Museum** which has various relics from holy buildings around the city. It is in a fifteenth-century house from the Venetian period. There are many examples of fine stonework, the best being found on the tombs of the Dampierre family. The key is available from the library across the road.

Beyond the Lapidary Museum is the **Haidar Pasha mosque**, once St Catherine's cathedral, dating from the fourteenth century. It was converted to a mosque in 1571 and named after one of the generals in the Turkish army. It is now being restored. The Yeni Cami mosque, a little further north on the same street, has a similar history although it was destroyed in the eighteenth century and a new mosque was built.

Another mosque, that of **Aziz Efendi** lies behind Selimiye mosque. It is probably the oldest convent in the town and built in memory of Aziz Efendi, a Turkish martyr whose tomb lies inside along with those of two other unidentified people.

The **Museum of Barbarism** is in the new town on Mehmet Akif Caddesi. It has exhibits documenting the inter-communal troubles of 1963.

There are few large shops in the old town but rather small shops which have been there for years. They sell pottery, copper items and jewellery. There are many tailors and shoe shops where the visitor can get made-to-measure items in 24 hours. There is one modern area, the Galleria,which has various shops with a more European flavour. Fruit is sold from small hand carts all around the city.

Aditional Information

SOUTH NICOSIA

Accommodation

Details of hotels are available from the tourist office. Visitors should be aware that hotels in the centre of the old town may be very noisy.

Youth Hostel
13 Prince Charles Street
☎ 02 444808
Open: all year 7.30-10am, 4pm-11pm

Local Events

There are numerous cultural activities in Nicosia, recitals and major international sporting events

Late May
International trade fair with stands from all over the world.

28 June-1 July
Beer festival in the Carlsberg brewery grounds. There are displays of dancing and music and plenty of beer.

Late September
The Cyprus rally, which always attracts a large number of world-class drivers. The course starts and finishes in Nicosia.
Contact Cyprus Automobile Association ☎ 02 313232.

Last two weeks in September
Handicrafts exhibition at the Cyprus Handicrafts Centre, Athalassa Avenue.
There is the chance to see artisans at work on their particular crafts.
For further information
☎ 02 305024.

Places to Visit

Cyprus Archaeological Museum
☎ 02 302189
Open: Mon-Sat 9am-5pm, Sun 10am-1pm

Byzantine Museum
☎ 02 456781
Open: May-Sept Mon-Fri 9.30am-1pm, 2-5.30pm, Sat 9am-1pm; Oct-April Mon-Fri 9am-1pm, 2-5pm, Sat 9am-1pm

Folk Art Museum
☎ 02 463205
Open: all year Mon-Fri 8.30am-1pm, 2-4pm, Sat 8.30am-1pm

Leventis Municipal Museum
☎ 02 441475
Open: all year Tues-Sun 10am-4.30pm

National Struggle Museum
☎ 02 302465
Open: May-Sept Mon-Fri7.30am-1.30pm, 3-5pm 7.30am-1.30pm, Sat 7.30am-1.30pm; Oct-April 7.30am-2pm, 3-5pm, Sat 7.30am-1pm

Hadjigeorjakis House
Open: May-Sept Mon-Sat 7.30am-1.30pm; Oct-April Mon-Fri 7.30am-2pm, Sat 7.30am-1pm

Omerye Mosque
Open: all year Mon-Sat 9am-3pm

Famagusta Gate
☎ 02 430877

Cyprus Handicraft Service
Athalassa avenue
☎ 02 305024
Open: Mon-Fri 7.30am-2pm, Sat 7.30am-1pm
There is also a shop in Laiki Yitonia centre.

Sports

Bowling
Kykko Bowling
3½ miles (5km) from city centre
☎ 02 450085

Horse Riding
Lapatsa Sporting Centre
7 miles (11km) southwest of Nicosia
☎ 02 621201

Horse Racing
Nicosia Race Course
Just west of the city

Swimming
There are swimming pools at the
major hotels and it is possible to
apply for day membership.

Nicosia Olympic Pool
Near the Ministry of Agriculture

Shooting
Nicosia Shooting Club
Tseri 5miles (8km) south of the city
centre
☎ 02 482660

Tennis
Field Club (city centre)
Egypt Avenue
☎ 02 452041

Eleon Tennis Club
3 Ploutarchos Street
Engomi
☎ 02 449923
Also swimming pool

Lapatsa Sport Centre
Deftera 7 miles (11km) southwest
of Nicosia
☎ 02 621201

There is a fully equipped athletics
stadium 4 miles (6½km) southeast
of the city.

Fishing
A licence is required and available

from the Fisheries Department
13 Tagmatachiou Pouliou Street
☎ 02 330470
Athalassa Dam (in suburbs of
Nicosia)

Tourist Offices

Postal enquiries
18 Theodotou Street
PO BOX 4535

Laiki Yitonia
East of Eleftheria Square
☎ 02 444264

Transport

To Larnaca: Kallenos Bus Co,
    Leonidou St 34 ☎ 02 453560
To Limassol: Kemek Bus Co,
    Leonidou St ☎ 02 463989
To Limassol/Paphos: Costas Bus,
    Tripoli Bastion ☎ 02 464636
To Ayia Napa: Eman Bus, from
    Eleftheria square
There are also some services to the
Troodos resorts

Entertainment

Municipal Theatre
Museum Street

Various cultural activities including films and theatre are run by:
the British Council (Museum Ave),
the American Cultural Centre, the
German Goethe Institute and the
French Institute. Details from the
tourist office or the relevant
embassy.

There are numerous cinemas across
the city, some open air.

Emergencies

Nicosia General Hospital
☎ 02 451111
General emergency ☎ 199

NORTH NICOSIA

Northern Cyprus is not yet well equipped for the tourist and independent travel is therefore more difficult, but for the intrepid more rewarding.

Accommodation

There is little tourist accommodation in northern Nicosia, with most package deals being based on the coast. The tourist office may be able to help. There is one large hotel in Attaturk Square.

Places to Visit

Ethnographic Museum
Dervish Pasha Konagi
Open: May-Sept 9am-1.30pm,4.30-6.30pm; Oct-Apr 8am-1pm, 2.30-5pm

Handicraft Museum
Mevlevi Tekke
Girne Caddesi
Open: May-Sept 9am-1.30pm, 4.30-6.30pm, Oct-Apr 8.am-1pm, 2.30-5pm

Museum of Barbarism
Mehmet Akif Caddesi
Open: May-Sept 9am-1.30pm, 4.30-6.30pm; 8am-11.30am, 2.30-5.30pm

Lapidary Museum
Behind Selimye Mosque
Open: May-Sept 9am-1.30pm, 4.30-6.30pm; 8am-11.30am, 2.30-5.30pm

The smaller museums and sites are normally kept locked and do not have formal opening times but will be unlocked on request.

Visitors can enter mosques if they are suitably dressed. The most interesting are:

Arabahmet Mosque
Off Arasta street

Bedsten
Next to Selimiye mosque
Not open the the public, visitors have to peer through the fence.

Selimiye Mosque
Kirlizade Street

Kyrenia [Girne] Gate
Main entrance to the city from Kyrenia [Girne] and Famagusta [Gazimagusa]

Transport

There are buses to Kyrenia [Girne] and Famagusta [Gazimagusa]

Tourist Office

Opposite the old British High Commission, on the road out to Kyrenia [Girne].
Open; April-Sept Mon-Fri 8am-2pm, 2.30-5pm; Oct-March Mon-Fri 8am-1pm, 2.30-5pm

Emergencies

Police ☎ 020 83411
First Aid ☎ 020 71441

10

FAMAGUSTA [GAZIMAGUSA] AND THE KARPAS

The road from Nicosia to Famagusta [*Gazimagusa*] runs across the flat Mesaoria plain which, in summer, is very dusty and barren. The road follows the line of the old camel trail.

This area contains one the most famous archaeological site on the island: *Salamis*. It also contains one of the strangest and perhaps saddest places on the island: the modern town of Famagusta. Once it was the tourist centre of Cyprus but now it is a ghost town, inaccessible to all but the military, having been taken over by the Turks in their 1974 invasion but not settled by them.

The city can be reached on two roads from Nicosia, the old and new. The new is 34 miles (54½km) and bypasses the villages on the route. The old road leads past **Tymbou**, now Ercan airfield which has flights to Turkey. The villages have few items of specific interest, their churches tend to be abandoned, although they are typical ramshackle Cypriot settlements. Famagusta lies 38 miles (61km) away on this route.

Famagusta, also known by its Turkish name of *Gazimagusa* and its Greek name of *Ammochostos* (buried in sand), lies on the east coast. There are some ferry services to Turkey from the town. The city contains two distinct areas, the old town with its considerable history within its walls and Varosha, which used to be the tourist centre of the island and its third largest city, which is now abandoned to the military. Visitors arriving by sea enter the old city along Liman Yolu Sokaki which leads into Istiklal Caddesi which is the main shopping street. The main beach of Famagusta is inaccessible.

As with so many of these towns its early history is obscure. Some claim that King Ptolemy of Egypt founded the city in 285BC and there are some indications of Roman occupation, but the main settlement in the area at that period was always *Salamis* up the coast.

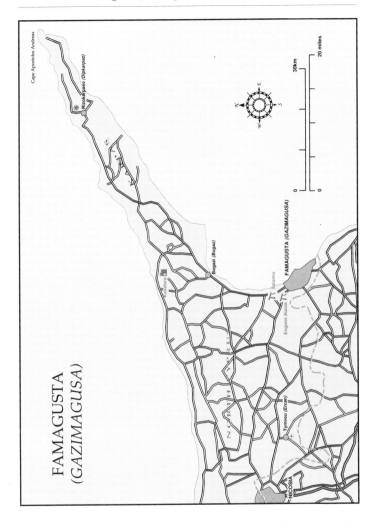

Only when *Salamis* was abandoned did Famagusta become a settlement and even then for about six hundred years it was only a small fishing village.

However, by 1300 as Cyprus became a major trading nation, the attractions of Famagusta's fine harbour led to its transformation into one of the most important ports, not only in Cyprus, but also in the Mediterranean. It was during the Lusignan period that most of the defences were built. The period between 1300 and 1400 was very much a golden age for Famagusta with many rich traders settling here and its fine deep water harbour was improved. The city then gained a reputation for sin and vice and as a centre for scandalous living. There was some trouble between the Venetians and the Genoese until the Venetians took full control in 1489. The Venetians put massive efforts into rebuilding and extending the city walls.

There was peace until 1570 when the Turks laid siege to the town and after a great deal of bloodshed, when over 50,000 Turks died, they succeeded in capturing it. The Venetian governor Bragadino was tricked into signing a a truce and many of his troops were slaugthered when they came out of the city, believing that they had been guaranteed safe passage. The governor himself though, suffered the worst fate as the Turks put him on display and then flayed him alive and stuffed his skin with straw. These grisly remains are now in an urn in Venice, placed there after the Turks had exhibited him around the Middle East.

After the battle, the town declined; the Muslims lived inside the walls, while the Christians gathered outside, although both communities lived in squalid conditions. When the British took over in 1878, they dredged the harbour which brought trade and renewal to the town. This prosperity continued after independence when Famagusta became the centre of the tourist industry and its long sandy beach was marked by a huge number of hotels. But after the 1974 invasion the new town was sealed off to all but the military and the old town resettled by the Turkish community. Even the old town is very quiet these days. There are a few restaurants and hotels but the main tourist centres are a few miles up the coast.

π The Venetian walls, 2 miles (3.5km) long, are the most striking part of the old city. They are 50 ft (15m) high and 26ft (8m) wide in places and one can walk along them, passing the fifteen bastions. There are reminders of all the various occupants of the city inscribed on the walls: carvings from the Lusignan period, Genoese coats of arms and Turkish inscriptions. The east wall overlooks the harbour while the remaining walls are surrounded by a moat, which is now an empty and quiet place to walk.

❀ The **Land Gate**, at the southwest corner of the walls used to be the main entrance to the city. Its arch is 30ft (9m) high and the Rivettina bastion stands at its side with a complex of dungeons and guardrooms and it was the scene of heavy fighting in the siege of 1571.

There are four smaller bastions along the west wall: Diocaro, Moratto, Pulacazoro and San Louca. Then comes the immense
❀ **Martinengo Bastion**, named after a Venetian commander and is one

of the finest examples of military architecture in the Mediterranean. It deterred the Turkish invaders who decided to launch their assault on the city at a more vulnerable part of the city. The walls are 13-20ft (4-6m) in width and are best seen from the moat. The remainder of the northern walls are defended by the Del Mozzo and Diamente bastions.

Passing the small Signoria bastion heading towards the sea front, the visitor reaches the Citadel or **Othello's Tower**. There is a story, admittedly unlikely, that Christopher Moro, a Venetian Governor, was the inspiration for Shakespeare's *Othello* which has its main action in Cyprus. All the evidence suggests that Shakespeare based his play on a story by an Italian writer, Cinthio, although Shakespeare changed and embellished the basic story of the wife of a Moorish army captain who dies amid plots and jealousy. What is remarkable about *Othello* is the extremely evocative atmosphere created, which gives a very strong indication of what life was like in Venetian Famagusta and highlights the ever-present threat of Turkish invasion which the town lived through and to which it finally succumbed.

The citadel was built in the fourteenth century by the Lusignans and has four towers. It was surrounded by a seawater moat. The entrance is through one of the round towers which has the winged lion of St Mark carved above it. The courtyard is surrounded by many chambers and the great hall. Inside the great hall, in the keystone of one of the vaulted arches, is the cross of Jerusalem. There are canon balls embedded in the walls of the courtyard. It is worth a visit for the excellent views of the harbour from the battlements.

Further south is the **Sea Gate**, best seen from inside the town, and which is another fine piece of military engineering. The Turks added the iron gates. Next, at the southern end of the seafront, is the **Djamboulat Gate** (Arsenal Gate). This is where the Turkish general Djamboulat Bey died in the siege and was the site of some very fierce fighting over many months and the loss of 20,000 lives. Underneath the gate was the ammunition store which the Turks stormed and then blew up.

According to legend, Djamboulat, the Turkish commander died here on a particularly fiendish Venetian weapon, a windmill-like machine which had knife blades instead of sails. Its constant revolving provided a seemingly impenetrable defence until Djamboulat threw himself at the machine stopping it and allowing his troops to pass through although he, of course, came to an extremely unpleasant end.

He then became a hero throughout the Turkish Empire and was

buried here in a simple tomb on a raised platform. The bastion is now a museum. The exhibits include Turkish costumes from a variety of historical periods, swords and a decorated sixteenth-century copy of the *Koran*.

Camposanto, Andrusz and Santa Napa are the remaining and smaller bastions. Those walking round the walls should take extra care as there are many unguarded steep parts.

There are many fine buildings in the town itself including an eleventh-century Gothic church, once St Nicholas Cathedral, now **Lala Mustapha Pasha mosque**, named after the commander of the Turkish army of 1571. It has an impressive west front in a simple austere style. It used to be the place where Lusignan Kings were crowned and King James II and James III are buried here. It is now a mosque, marked by twin towers without tops next to a minaret.

Inside are interesting windows including a rose window in the centre of the church. Other additions were two chapels. The cathedral was damaged in the Turkish siege and in an earthquake of 1735 so its full splendour can no longer be fully appreciated. In its heyday it invited comparisons with some of the great French cathedrals. Outside is a tree which is supposed to be 700 years old and two granite columns between which the Venetian governor was flayed. Across the way is the Archbishop's palace and a Venetian loggia and a fountain.

The **Sinan Pasha mosque** is a little to the north and was built as the church of Saint Peter and Paul in 1368. It was converted in 1571 to a mosque and and then in 1964 it was restored as a public building, first as the town hall and nowadays serves as a public library. In the courtyard is the tomb of Mehmet Efendi a famous eighteenth-century Turkish diplomat.

Close by is a Lusignan palace with four columns, probably from *Salamis*, on its façade. The Turks used it as a prison after the siege, and its most illustrious inmate was the poet Nemuk Kemal (1840-88) who was exiled here after allegedly insulting the sultan. All seems to have been forgiven and the building now houses the **Nemuk Kemal Museum**. There is also a bust of him in the square.

Curiously for a city which has such a long Muslim tradition there are a large number of churches in Famagusta, although many have now fallen into disrepair or are inaccessible due to the presence of the miltary. One interesting building is the **Nestorian church** near the Moratto Bastion. It was built in 1350 for the Nestorian (Syrian) community of the city but was used as a Greek Orthodox church until 1963, with an interlude when it served as a camel stable.

On the seaward side of the old city is the church of **St George of the**

Lala Mustapha Pasha mosque, once St Nicholas cathedral, Famagusta [Gazimagusa]

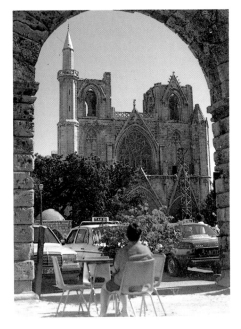

The ruins of Salamis, one of the ten City Kingdoms of Cyprus

Greeks which was once an orthodox cathedral. It has wall paintings on the three apses and is built in both Gothic and Byzantine styles.

North of Famagusta

The site of *Engomi Alasia* is important archaeologically and there is a wide spread of ruins although the amateur may find it hard to distinguish much of any real interest. It lies 5 miles (8km) north of Famagusta. The remains date from the seventeenth century BC and the settlement was probably a copper exporting city. It suffered extensive damage in a fire and then in the earthquake of the twelfth century BC and was then abandoned.

Visitors enter the north gate and can see the sanctuary of the Horned God whose statue was found along with a clay tablet inscribed with Cypro-Minoan script which has not yet been decoded. There are also a few houses called respectively: Building 18, House of the Pillar, and the House of the Bronzes where many bronze artefacts were found.

There are a few beaches on the route up to Salamis, mainly around the hotels, including Palm Beach Hotel, Clapsides Beach and Salamis Bay Hotel.

The site of *Salamis*, 6 miles (9½km) north of Famagusta, is one of the most significant in Cyprus and perhaps in the Mediterranean. Its earliest history is unclear but it was a City Kingdom from at least the eleventh century BC, being the island's capital. One legend has it that it was built by Teukros, the son of the king of Salamis in Greece, who was exiled by his father for having failed to prevent Ajax, his brother, committing suicide. Teukros turned up in Cyprus at the end of the Trojan war and created Salamis. It certainly was a good place for a settlement with its natural harbour and good defensive position.

The city grew to prominence when *Engomi* was abandoned and for a thousand years it was the most important Cypriot city. It was one of the most powerful and prosperous of the City Kingdoms on the island and its kings were prominent in the various uprisings against the Persians. King Evagoras was one with particular ambition. He planned to unite all the Greek kings and with the help of the Athenians remove the Persians from the island. However, even his formidable diplomatic skills failed to bring the required unity and he died with his ambition unrealised.

It remained the richest city on the island even when the Romans moved the capital to Paphos. Its harbour was the central trading post of the Middle East through which most of the island's exports passed and *Salamis* was connected by road to most of the other major sites on the island. However in 76AD earthquakes caused damage and it was ruined by tidal waves in 400AD. The Byzantine Emperor Constantine rebuilt it and called it *Constantia* and it became the island's capital again and it prospered until it was sacked by the Arabs in the seventh century.

The first excavations took place in 1880 and revealed very extensive ruins which had been well preserved due to them being buried under sand for so many years. The site is very large and divided into two by the road and visitors can explore on foot or by car. It is a confusing site and it is best to wander, identifying the buildings as they are encountered rather than following a set plan. The south and west of the town were originally surrounded by defensive walls and an outer set of walls was added in the seventh century in a vain attempt to keep out Arab raiders. The interior walls are still visible in parts.

The *Gymnasium* is the most photographed part of the site and it is impressive with its tall pillars which were built by the Roman and then again by the archaeologists. It served as the exercise ground and baths for the Romans, suggesting they had plenty of time for leisure activities. Clearly its construction was a major undertaking, as the marble was brought from Greece and Italy and then had to be manouevred from the harbour to the site.

Nearby is a complex of buildings which contained the baths in rooms off a maze of corridors and different rooms. In the west hall the heating system can be seen particularly clearly. The furnaces needed enormous numbers of slaves to keep them stoked up with fuel; the heated air then passed along the hypocausts. The Romans had an incredibly sophisticated plumbing system and the remains of this and an aqueduct which brought water to the town are still visible.

A curiosity of the area is the number of headless statues and there are numerous theories why they should have been so decapitated. One is that the Romans, after they had converted to Christianity, objected to the pagan statues and removed the heads. Alternatively they might have been removed centuries later in the Renaissance period by antiques merchants who were capitalising on a lucrative trade in such items.

The *Theatre* lies just south of the *Gymnasium* and is another impressive structure. It has been well restored, despite the fact that many of its original decorations and statues have disappeared. It was first built in 200AD and the tiers of seats rise up to 67ft (20m) in fifty rows and could originally seat 15,000 people. Apparently it had a channel in the centre of the orchestra pit through which the blood from sacrifices could drain away.

The *Agora,* just beyond a large cistern, is one of the largest of such market places in the Mediterranean. At the entrance was a large public building behind which were the city walls. On each side are stumps of columns and there once was a temple at one end, although only the podium is now visible here. There is a frieze with Latin inscriptions which tell of the restoration of the building in 22BC.

There were three Christian basilicas on the site, none of which are easily identifiable. *Salamis* is important in Christian history because it was the birthplace of St Barnabas who later returned with St Paul to bring Christianity to the island. The largest church was that of St Epiphianos. All that remains are two rows of stumps of columns and a semicircle where the apse used to be. The tomb of St Epiphianos remains but his body was moved to Constantinople. Campana Petra church stands close to the harbour and some of its walls are still standing. There is also a Byzantine church with its apse still visible as well as some of the fonts used in baptism.

The port is a mile (1½km) away where the remnants of a jetty are visible. It was made from huge stone blocks and swimmers will be able to take a closer look.

On the other side of the road are the royal tombs and *Necropolis* where excavations continue. Many of the tombs were looted but nonetheless significant discoveries have been made here. This area, known as the Tomb of the Kings, contains one tomb called St Catherine's Prison which is made from large blocks of stone and was probably used as a chapel. Numerous legends have grown up about this tomb. One is that of Catherine, the daughter of a king of *Salamis,* was converted to Christianity and this offended her uncle who had, by this point, become king. He ordered her to keep out of sight in this room where she lived for the rest of her life. An alternative version claims that Catherine shut herself up voluntarily out of devotion to Christ. Certainly the chambers are stark and somewhat sad.

Many of the other tombs contain the skeletons of horses which were buried in a sacrifice after the death of their owner. There are also remnants of chariots and bronze blinkers used on the horses. On the floor of Tomb 50 are the skeletons of two horses yoked together.

The Royal Tombs are some of the finest on the island, while in the *Necropolis* itself ordinary citizens were buried in plain tombs cut out of the rock. There is a small museum close by, which has exhibits outlining the finds and the burial rites of the community.

One mile from *Salamis*, opposite the Royal Tombs, is St Barnabas monastery. The present building was constructed in 1756 but there had been a church on the site since the fifth century to house the bones of St Barnabas which were discovered in a cave after the local archbishop had a dream which revealed the saint's whereabouts. This sequence of events is shown in a painting on the wall. The church is rather ornate in contrast to the simple tomb a short walk away.

The Karpas [*Kirpasa*]

The Karpas [*Kirpasa*] is one of the most remote areas of the island stretching out along the long panhandle which is such a distinctive feature of the geography of Cyprus. It is particularly wild and natural area with few facilities for the tourists. Today it has some Greek enclaves, small communities which have not moved south and remain a continuing source of controversy.

The route runs close to the coast from *Salamis* to Bogaz and is a good road with fine scenery. **Bogaz** is a small seaside resort with a hotel. It is known for its lacemaking and in spring for its wild flowers. The road then turns inland and while equally impressive is now characterised by narrow bends and becomes a more difficult drive.

The visitor can take an excursion to **Kantara Castle**; its name means escarpment in Arabic, and it is found just north of the village of Kantara. It lies at a height of just over 2,000ft (610m) offering spectacular views of the bay and occasionally the mountains of Turkey. The castle is last in the trio of the grand Kyrenia castles, the others being St Hilarion and Buffavento.

Its earliest remains are from 900AD and it was captured by Richard the Lionheart when he was pursuing Isaac Comnenos in 1191. The Lusignans took it over and expanded it to serve as a major fortification. However, the Venetians dismantled most of it, believing the old castle style was no longer a useful military defence. It then fell into ruins although it was inhabited by Simeon the Hermit during 1815-75. The outer wall is still intact and the visitor enters through the barbican and up some steps into the tower. Also visible are the guardroom and storerooms as well as the latrine — it seems that the castle had a good drainage system. From the tower there are spectacular views through a Gothic window. There is another tower in the northeast of the grounds and the remains of some of the corridors are still visible.

Three miles (5km) below Kantara castle is **Kaplica** village and its beach. There is an abandoned hotel with a long stretch of sand.

Next on the peninsula is **Ayios Thyrsos [*Florya Gazinosu*]** with a restaurant with good views over the sea. There are three Greek churches and a harbour used by local fishermen.

Rizokarpaso [*Dipkarpaz*] is the market centre for the area. Some claim that it was one of the six great cities of Cyprus but there is very little sign of that now. Its decline began after the 1570 invasion and its main trade was in mulberry leaves for silkworms. The village is now characterised by the remaining Greeks who live there. Three miles (5km) away is the ancient site of *Karpasia*. It was a Roman city and fragments of a mosaic from the church can be seen. There are also the remains of the Roman harbour.

The visitor can reach the very end of the panhandle to **Apostolos Andreas monastery** and a wonderful beach.

Additional Information

Places to Visit
Archaeological sites
There are standard opening times for archaeological sites in North Cyprus: May-Sept 9am-1.30pm, 4.30-6.30pm; Oct-April 8am-1pm, 2.30-5pm

Namik Kemal Museum
Kisla Sokagi
Famagusta [*Gazimagusa*]
Open: Tues-Sun May-Sept 9am-1.30pm, 4.30pm-6.30pm; Oct-Apr 8am-1pm, 2.30-5pm

The following buildings in Famagusta [*Gazimagusa*] tend not to have formal opening hours. If they are not open, ask at the nearest café for details of access:

Nestorian Church
North-east of Moratto bastion

St George of the Greeks
Mustapha Ersa Sokagi

St Nickolas of the Greeks
Lala Mustapha Pasha Mosque

Sinan Pasha Mosque
Sinan Pasa Sokagi

Sport
There are few formal facilities for sport in the north although the hotels may have some provision for watersports and a few have tennis courts.

Transport
There are buses from Famagusta [*Gazimagusa*] to Nicosia [*Lefkosa*] and there are also some buses which will stop at *Salamis*.

Tourist Office
Opposite the Monument of Victory just outside the city walls, Famagusta [*Gazimagusa*]
Open: Apr-Sept Mon-Fri 8am-2pm; Oct-Mar 8am-1pm, 2.30pm-5pm

Emergencies
Police ☎ 036 65310
First Aid ☎ 036 62876

11

KYRENIA [GIRNE] AND THE SURROUNDING AREA

Kyrenia (now known by its Turkish name of *Girne*) is a small harbour town with a strong history and lies in the shadow of the Kyrenia [*Besparmak*] Hills on the north coast of the island. Since the Turkish invasion in 1974 it has escaped some of the excesses of development seen in the south, although it is increasingly catering for tourists. Venetian mansions still line the harbour, but these have now been converted into cafés and restaurants. These, along with the castle at the far end, form a picturesque panorama.

The town is at least three thousand years old and was founded by the Achaeans as part of an ancient city kingdom. It was an important Greek colony from 1,200-1,000BC. Later, around 56BC, the Romans took it over and called it *Corineum*, but as with the Greeks neither left much of a mark. Like the island's other coastal towns it suffered frequent attacks from seaborne raiders in the Middle Ages and these led to the construction of the walls and the towers. The Byzantines built the castle which was reasonably successful, both in warding off pirate raids and a major assault by the Genoese in 1374. The Venetians then took over the island and further strengthened the city walls and the castle but they proved useless when the Turks attacked in 1570 and Kyrenia quickly surrendered.

It then was left to fall into decline until the arrival of the British who improved its facilities, building hospitals and extending the harbour, so that it became one of the favourite haunts of the British. Colonials and some long-time residents remain today. Lawrence Durrell lived at nearby Bellapais and described its charms in *Bitter Lemons*. The book is a vivid account both of the curious expatriate life and of the culture of the Cypriots. It is also a haunting and bitter outline of the trauma of the EOKA terror campaign which eventually drove him from the island.

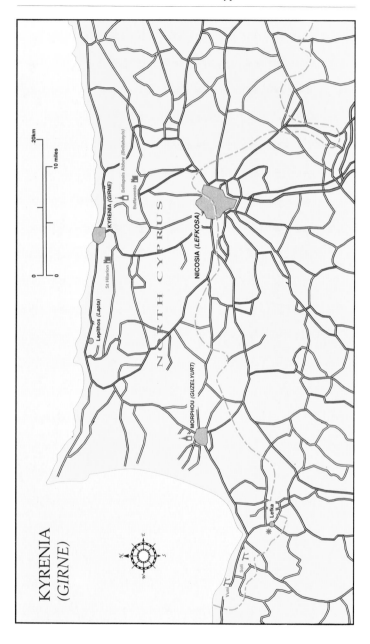

KYRENIA
(GIRNE)

NORTH CYPRUS

KYRENIA (GIRNE)

NICOSIA (LEFKOSA)

MORPHOU (GUZELYURT)

Lepithos (Lapta)

St Hilarion

Bellapais Abbey (Bellabayis)

Buffavento

Lefka

Vuni

Soli

0   10 miles
0   20km

The harbour at Kyrenia [Girne]

Bellapais Abbey

In 1974 the Turkish army landed just west of here and went on to occupy 40 per cent of the island. A new port has been built to accommodate the ferry service to Turkey 43 miles (70km) away. The main street is Hummiyet Caddesi where shops, restaurants and the 'bus station can be found.

The harbour is clearly the centre of the town with restaurants and cafés lined along the quays. At the far end of the harbour is **Kyrenia Castle,** the main site of interest. There may have been a fortress here as early as the first or second century BC which was then occupied by the Romans, although there is no conclusive proof of this. The current structure was probably constructed in the ninth century to protect the Byzantine city. The first confirmed reference to the castle is in 1191 when it was attacked by Guy de Lusignan. At this point the city was totally enclosed by walls stretching from the castle to the tower on Humiyet Caddesi to the one by the Archangelos church. However, these walls are no longer visible.

The Lusignans made full use of the castle as a prison and Peter I's wife used it to imprison his mistress, to whom she had understandably taken a violent dislike. It seems his wife also took revenge on her husband as he was found in bed with his head hacked off. The castle became increasingly favoured as the royal residence and as a refuge when other parts of the island were proving dangerous.

The Venetians took over in 1464 and made extensive additions to strengthen the castle. Thus the remains of three castles are visible: Byzantine, Lusignan and Venetian. The Turks captured it without a fight and the tomb of the victorious Turkish general, Sadik Pasha, is in the entrance hall of the castle. The British used it as a prison until 1950 when it was handed over to the Department of Antiquities and restored, only to be used again as a prison during the EOKA rising.

The castle walls are 24ft (7m) thick. Visitors go in through the northwest entrance near the moat which was once filled with water and then pass along a corridor marked by a Lusignan coat of arms. There is also a small Byzantine church with marble columns. The south and west wall, northwest and southeast towers are of Venetian construction. Around the courtyard are the royal apartments.

In the guardroom is the **Shipwreck Museum**, with a trading ship which sailed the seas during the reign of Alexander the Great and sank around 300BC a mile out from the harbour. The ship was found in the late 1960s in water 60ft (18m) deep. It is 47ft (14m) long and had often been repaired, hardly surprising in view of its great age, as it was 80 years old when it sank. A wide range of objects were collected from the ship which give interesting insights into the lives of the sailors. Numerous cooking implements have been found including salt pots, spoons and oil jars and a bronze cooking cauldron. The main cargo was wine, mainly from Rhodes, stored in 4,000 amphorae; there were also almonds in jars and twenty-nine millstones.

The shell of the vessel was raised from the sea but its reconstruction proved to be extremely difficult and took six years. After its completion it was placed in preservative fluid and from the viewing gallery visitors can now see the ship, fully restored. There are also photographs of the original diving expedition.

Just the other side of the castle is a sandy beach where the sea tends to be calm, even when it is rough elsewhere. Apart from this bay the shore in the town is somewhat rocky which makes swimming difficult and visitors would do better to head east or west of the town where there are many fine sandy beaches.

By the harbour, on Pasabahce Street, is the **Folk Art Museum** which contains various handicrafts and furniture from the eighteenth century. The three-storey building overlooks the water and used to be a barn and grain store. On the ground floor are agricultural tools, large earthenware pots and weaving looms. The second floor represents a small sitting room. On the third floor there are bedspreads, tablecloths and other examples of embroidery as well as kitchen implements and traditional costumes.

Just inland from the harbour is the mosque of **Cafer Pasa**, dating from the Ottoman occupation, with a fine minaret.

At the opposite end of the town is the **Decorative Arts Museum** which has paintings and crafts from the Far East along with some Chinese porcelain.

Routes out of Kyrenia

One of the most spectacular sites near Kyrenia is **Bellapais Abbey**, which lies 4 miles (6½km) southeast of the town heading towards Nicosia in the foothills of the Pentadaktylos [*Besparmak*] range. The abbey, a fine example of Gothic architecture, was founded in 1200 by Amery de Lusignan and then received substantial donations from Hugh lll who was buried there. Hugh IV spent his life here and added some royal apartments, but after his death the buildings became dilapidated. It was sacked by the Turks in 1570, turned into a military hospital by the British and then finally restored in 1912.

The main entrance is in the southwest through a fourteenth-century arched gateway into the forecourt and the thirteenth-century church, which is the earliest part of the monastery. It is possible to climb up a spiral stair to the roof of the abbey to take in the wonderful views of the mountains and the surrounding buildings.

From the forecourt the visitor enters the cloister which is decorated with many carvings of animals and human figures. The refectory has a very beautiful interior, with a vaulted roof supported by fourteen pillars. The remains of the benches upon which the monks sat are visible. The room is lit by a rose window at one end and six windows on the north side which have impressive views of the coast below. There is a pulpit ingeniously built into the wall. The kitchens were sited just outside the refectory.

❋ In the village of Bellapais is the Tree of Idleness mentioned by Lawrence Durrell in *Bitter Lemons*. It is now surrounded by cafés and is a pleasant place to sit and relax.

🏰 Rejoining the main Nicosia road and then turning right is the road to **St Hilarion Castle** one of the three great castles of the Kyrenia hills which were built to look out over the sea and provide early warning of the approach of invaders. It stands at an altitude of 2,220ft (670m) and has spectacular views down to the coast. Some say the castle served as the inspiration for Walt Disney's castle in *Snow White and the Seven Dwarfs*.

It is named after the hermit Hilarion who lived here a thousand years ago in a small monastery. According to legend demons used to cling to the mountain until they were banished by the power of Hilarion's prayer. The Lusignans then took over and strengthened the castle and used it as a summer retreat. The castle walls are a quarter of a mile (400m) in length with nine towers.

It was the focus of numerous inter-Lusignan battles for the crown and possession passed frequently from one side to the other, but it always remained one of the royal family's favourite residences. There is the story of a particularly grisly incident when Prince John, believing his Bulgarian mercenaries had been disloyal, threw them one by one over the precipice to their deaths. The castle was besieged by the Genoese in one of their many attempts to gain footholds in the island, but when the Venetians took over it became less important despite its strategic position and it was left in ruins. However, it was the scene of fierce fighting in the 1974 invasion when the Turks used it as an observation post and the area is still occupied by the military although the castle is open to visitors.

The entrance to the castle is through a gatehouse leading into the lower ward. From here the garrison's quarters and the stables are visible. The upper storey has fine views of the walls and the tenth-century Byzantine church. Up the stairs are the royal apartments which have now been converted into a restaurant.

It is possible to reach the upper ward taking a path from the middle ward. It does, however require a certain agility to reach St John's Tower which lies on a rocky crag with steep drops on three sides. At

The rocky peaks of the Pentadaktylos [Besparmark] Hills

A quiet beach on the northern coast

the top is a cistern, arched gateway, the kitchens and more of the royal apartments. From the Queen's Room there is a magnificent outlook over the sea. The hills all around the the castle offer some spectacular views and places for picnics and walks.

Also in the area is **Buffavento Castle**, beyond Ayios Chrysostomos monastery and 8 miles (13km) south east of Kyrenia. The castle like the others lies high in the hills. The road passes through Gungos and close to the Ayios Chrysostomos monastery now occupied by the miltary. The final 1½ miles (2½km) from the village are not really passable for ordinary cars and one has to proceed on foot to the castle on a fairly steep path.

Buffavento is less well preserved than the other fortresses but it is the highest of the three at 2,600ft (790m) and therefore offers some of the best views looking over to the village of Catalkoy and in the distance, to Kyrenia itself. The castle's name means 'blown by wind'.

Its early history is unclear but it was probably built in the twelfth century and the garrison then survived until the Venetian period. Richard I paid a brief visit when the castle played an important part in his capture of the island from Comnenos, the then ruler of the island, who sent his daughter to shelter here for safety but who was then captured. The Lusignan King James is supposed to have used it as a prison and the Venetians established a garrison here for a while but later abandoned it and concentrated on their coastal defences.

The ruins cover two storeys with the Lusignan gatehouse leading into the lower wards. There are steps up to the top ward with the remains of a chapel but as the castle is in a state of dilapidation the visitor will not be able to make out much of the original structure.

While Kyrenia itself does not have many good beaches it is possible to find some fine stretches of sand west of the town. The first is **Riviera Mocamp**, 2½ miles (4km) away and signposted from the main road. There is a campsite here and there are plans to develop the area further. Next is **Five Mile** or **Golden Rock Beach**. It is possible to drive right down to the sand and the sea is shallow and suitable for children. There is a small rocky island just offshore to which one can wade. 7½ miles (12km) west of Kyrenia is **Mare Monte**, a tourist beach for which an entrance charge is made to cover the cost of cleaning the sand. There is a hotel and restaurant above the beach, which can be busy.

The village of **Lapithos [*Lapta*]** is 6 miles (10km) west of Kyrenia and left of the main road up in the hills, but it overlooks the beach from a distance. A perennial spring ensures that the surrounding land is extremely fertile and the area is famous for its orange and lemon groves. There has been a settlement here since 654AD and the village was once a Roman City Kingdom.

The main road then turns south with rough tracks off to Morphou [*Guzelyurt*] Bay which is characterised by long strips of shingle which are remote and far from any tourist trappings or facilities. There is extensive agricultural production with the main crops being citrus fruits and strawberries.

Morphou [*Guzelyurt*] is the only substantial town in the area and is characterised by a confusing maze of streets. The best place to start any exploration is the town square where there is the Byzantine monastery of Ayios Mamas. It has been extensively rebuilt, including the addition of its central dome. Its west door has some historic graffiti including inscriptions by the French consul recording his visit in 1753. There are numerous icons from different periods especially from the Venetian era. Various coats of arms from the same period are also visible.

The tomb of Ayias Mamas is found at the northern end of the church. The holes in it were made by the Turks in 1570s who hoped the sarcophagus would contain treasure, but they were disappointed. According to legend Ayias Mamas lived in a cave and felt that this should have exempted him from taxes. The taxman was not impressed and he was arrested and taken to Nicosia to explain himself. On the way they encountered a lion, an unlikely resident of Cyprus, the saint subdued the lion which was about to attack a lamb and then persuaded the lamb to act as his mount until they reached Nicosia. The Lusignan duke in charge of tax collection was so impressed by all this that Mamas was excused paying taxes. This feat of tax evasion, as much as any piety, seems to have been responsible for the reverence with which he was then received by the local peasants. Next door to the church is the Archaeology and Natural History Museum which contains finds from the Late Cypriot Age.

South of Morphou [*Guzelyurt*] is the town of **Lefka [*Lefke*]**, lying in the foothills of the Troodos mountains.This is a another fertile region, irrigated by the melting snows of the mountains. It is known for its citrus fruits and there is a reservoir just outside the town which is pleasant for a picnic. In the town is the mosque of Piri Osman Pasa whose tomb can be found in the cemetery.

In this region are two important archaeological sites. *Soli* was founded in 6BC and was one of the ten City Kingdoms and played a major role in the opposition to the Persians, holding out for four months against their siege. In Roman times it was an important copper centre and a substantial settlement. The *Theatre* was built in 2AD and is still visible, carved out of the hillside. It had seventeen tiers of seats and has been restored. There are also remains of of an

Agora, *Acropolis* and a basilica which has a well preserved mosaic floor with depictions of birds.

It was attacked by Arab raiders during the seventh century which led to it being abandoned. Much of its stone was used to help build the Suez Canal which has made the ruins less visible. The first excavations took place in the 1930s and revealed temples to Aphrodite and to Isis.

The other site is the palace of *Vuni*, up a steep road 5½ miles (9km) from **Karavostasi** [*Gemikonagi*], on a plateau at an altitude of 923ft (277m). It has some very good views out over the sea. The site was first excavated in 1928-9 when some remains from 5BC were uncovered, including baths, but only low walls are visible today.

The main site was built on three terraces which seem to reflect three different periods of occupation. At the top of the hill are ruins from 5BC including a temple to Athena. On the second level were the palace and holy buildings. Seven steps lead down into a court around which there once was a series of 137 rooms on two storeys, including a kitchen, bathroom and a granary. The lowest section contained residential buildings. Just northeast of here were the baths. The city was destroyed by the Persians in 380BC.

East of *Vuni* is the village of **Limnitis** with a small island offshore where Neolithic remains have been found. It is not far from here to the Attila line dividing the island, thus making Polis and the far west inaccessible from this side of the border.

East of Kyrenia

There are several good beaches east of Kyrenia and the further east one goes the more isolated the area until one reaches the Karpas, the long panhandle of Cyprus, described in the Famagusta chapter.

Three miles (5km) east of Kyrenia is **Karakoumi [*Karakum*]** with a track down to the beach just outside the village. It is a pretty bay in a horseshoe shape which makes it a sheltered place. **Acapulco Beach**, named after the restaurant at its far end, is next along the shore. It is a long sandy stretch and safe for children and is popular at weekends. Some Neolithic pottery was found in an archaeologoical site by the restaurant. Another beach, which can be somewhat windswept, lies a little further along the main road.

12 miles (19km) east of Kyrenia is the longest sandy beach on the north coast. It is easy to miss as it is not visible from the main road. A track leads down to the sea through the dunes. Further along the coast is **Alakati Beach**, is a pleasant bay 13 miles (21km) east of Kyrenia where there is an interesting rock formation standing up as a pillar on the headland.

18 miles (29km) east of Kyrenia in a valley is the twelfth-century Antiphonitis church. It can be reached on foot from the village of **Bahceli** but this a strenuous walk. An alternative is to take the rough road via **Esentepe**. The church has four columns which support a large dome. There were additions made by the Lusignans in the fourteenth century and the loggia was added in the fifteenth century. Its paintings date from the twelfth century, but may be difficult to gain access to the interior of the church

Additional Information

Accommodation
There are no youth hostels or official campsites, but camping is possible at Riviera Mocamp west of Kyrenia [*Girne*] and Onur near Famagusta [*Gazimagusa*].
Lists of hotels are available from the tourist office; bed and breakfast is available in many towns.

Places to Visit
Shipwreck Museum
Kyrenia Castle
Kyrenia [*Girne*]

Folk Art Musuem
Pasabahce Street
Kyrenia [*Girne*]

Archaeology and Natural History Museum
Next to the church
Morphou [*Guzelyurt*]

The above museums have the standard North Cyprus opening times: May-September Tues-Sat 9am-1.30pm, 4.30-6.30pm; October-April 8am-1pm, 2.30-5pm

Bellapais
The exterior of the abbey can be visited in daylight hours, closed for siesta. The inside can be visited by special request, contact the custodian.

St Hilarion Castle
Open: 8am-6pm

Buffavento Castle

Sport
Walking
Hill walking is possible in the Kyrenia hills but walkers should avoid military areas.

Riding
Karaglanogolu ☎ 52855

Tennis
There are public courts to the west of the Nicosia road and at the Mare Monte Hotel 6 miles to the west of Kyrenia.

Tourist Office
Fehmi Ercan Cad
☎ 521 45
Open: May-Aug Mon 7.30am-6pm, Tues-Fri 7.30am-2pm; Sep-April Mon-Fri 8am-5.50pm

Transport
Minibuses go to Nicosia [*Lefkosa*] and Morphou [*Guzelyurt*] from the bus station on Humiyet Caddesi in Kyrenia [*Girne*]. There are also service taxis between most towns.

Emergencies
Kyrenia [*Girne*]
Fire: ☎ 52014
Police: ☎ 52125
Ambulance: ☎ 52266

Fact File: Cyprus

The island of Cyprus is divided into two: the Greek Cypriot southern part and the Turkish northern sector half. Where practice varies significantly the entries are divided into South and North. Details for North Cyprus are in italics.

Accommodation

South

There is a wide range of apartments and hotels available in Cyprus which are usually of a high standard. However, these are generally purpose-built for the pre-booked package holiday-maker and the more independent traveller may find accommodation difficult, although not impossible. All hotels are officially registered and listed in a booklet available from the tourist office. This gives a star rating (not always a reliable indicator of quality), details of facilities and prices.

There are campsites and youth hostels in or near all the major towns. It is also possible to stay in some of the monasteries although the facilities can be somewhat spartan and some do not allow women to stay. Rooms to rent, as found in the Greek islands, are gaining in popularity especially in the west of the island and in some of the villages.

North

Unlike the south, this part of the island is less overtly tourist oriented and there are fewer purpose-built resorts. Nonetheless there is a range of accommodation available which is rarely crowded. Again it is easier to come on a package deal arranged in advance, but bed and breakfast is available in some areas. The tourist office has details. There are campsites at Riviera Mocamp west of Kyrenia [Girne] and at Onur near Famagusta [Gazimagusa], but it is also possible to camp unofficially on many of the beaches.

Archaeological Sites

There are numerous archaeological sites across the island. The larger ones charge for entry and are fenced, but there are many smaller sites which are open to all. See individual chapters for details of opening times. Excavations are also continuing at many of the sites which can restrict access. Many of the best finds from the sites are in the Cyprus Museum in Nicosia.

Climate

Cyprus has long dry summers with guaranteed sunshine from May to October. In summer it is very hot: 38°C (100°F) inland, and 30°C (90°F) on the coast. From November to April it will be much cooler and gets dark quite early, although the main rain falls in December, January and February. April is a good time for

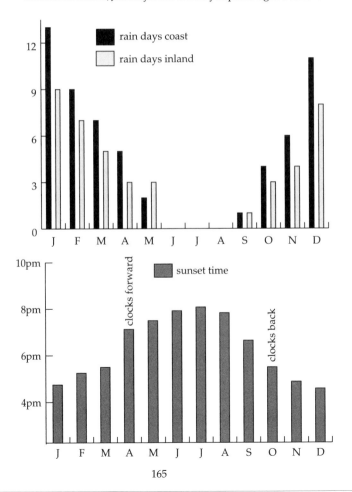

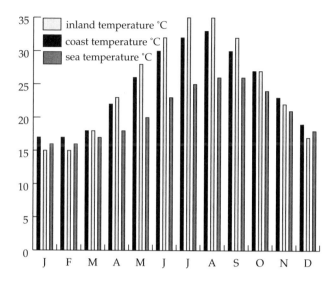

	inland temperature °C
	coast temperature °C
	sea temperature °C

nature lovers when the island is covered in flowers. The best time to go is probably May to September but July and August may be too hot for some tastes.

There are considerable differences between temperatures in the mountains and elsewhere. Even in summer night-time temperatures in the hills can be low and those planning to stay the night in the mountains should pack accordingly. However, daytime temperatures can still be very high and those walking or climbing should avoid July and August.

Currency and Credit Cards

South

The currency is Cyprus pounds (CY£) which is divided into 100 cents (c). There are coins of 20 cents, 10 cents, 5 cents, 2 cents, 1 cent and ½ cent. Notes are 50 cents, CY£1, CY£5 and CY£10. The change to cents from mils (1,000 to a pound) was relatively recent and prices may still be given in mils and occasionally, even more anachronistically, in shillings, a relic from British colonial days.

Up to CY£50 can be imported in currency. There is no limit on the amount of foreign currency, travellers cheques, etc which may be brought into the country. For amounts over 1,000 US dollars or equivalent a form D(NR) has to be filled in at customs.

There are numerous banks all over Cyprus and staff usually speak English.

Banking hours have recently been changed to stop Saturday opening. The standard opening times are Mon-Fri 8.15am-12 noon. However most banks offer exchange facilities for tourists for much longer hours, opening in the afternoon until 7pm and opening on a Saturday morning. Larnaca and Paphos airports both have exchange bureaux which are open all day.

Over 4,000 shops, restaurants and hotels accept the major credit cards, although these are in the main towns and resorts. Eurocheques are accepted in banks and some shops in resort areas.

Hotels have exchange facilities but rates are likely to be less favourable than in the banks.

Credit card holders can withdraw money from the following banks:

Visa: Bank of Cyprus, Cyprus Popular Bank, Hellenic Bank, Barclays Bank

Diners Club, Carte Blanche: Bank of Cyprus

MasterCard: Bank of Cyprus and National Bank of Greece

EuroCard: Bank of Cyprus and National Bank of Greece

Access Card: Bank of Cyprus and National Bank of Greece

American Express: Cyprus Popular Bank

North

The Turkish lira (TL) is the currency of northern Cyprus. There are coins for 50,100, 500 and 1,000TL, there are notes up to 100,000 lira. Many shops will also accept sterling, dollars and Greek Cypriot Pounds. There are no restrictions on the amount of currency that can be imported. Credit cards are accepted at some of the major hotel and shops but by no means universally.

It is possible to exchange money on the island itself, often with a better rate. Dollars and sterling are particularly welcome.

Bank opening hours: Mon-Sat summer 8am-12noon, winter 8.30am-12noon

Customs

All visitors to both south and north can import duty free:
250g of tobacco or equivalent, ie 200 cigarettes
1 litre of spirits, 0.75 litre of wine *(1 litre in North)*
0.30 litre of perfume
Other articles (except jewellery) up to a value of CY£50
The export of antiquities is forbidden.

Documents

South

Visas are not required for a 3-month stay except for visitors from some Eastern European countries, Israel, and Egypt. Visitors to the south can only enter through ports in the south, a stamp from the north prohibits entry and could cause problems in Greece.

Embassies and Consulates in Cyprus and abroad

Cyprus High Commission
93 Park Street
London W1Y 4ET
☎ 071 499 8272/4

British High Commission
Alexander Pallis Street
Nicosia
☎ 02 473131

Cyprus Embassy
2211 R St Northwest
Washington DC 20008
☎ 462 5772 or 462 0873

US Embassy
Dositheos & Therissos Street
Lycavitos
Nicosia
☎ 02 465151

Visiting the North

Travel across the border is restricted to one point at the Ledra Palace checkpoint in Nicosia under UN control. Visitors are only allowed to cross for one day and you must return by 5.30pm, no entry after 2pm. Clearance has to be gained from the Greek checkpoint and then visitors continue on foot to the Turkish checkpoint where various forms have to be signed and a fee of CY£1 paid. Hire cars are not allowed across the border. Visitors from the north are not allowed to cross into the south.

These regulations can change and the border has, at times, been closed completely.

North

Visas are not required. If asked, the immigration officer will stamp a piece of paper rather than the passport which can then be removed on departure and will avoid future problems for visitors to the south or to Greece.

Representative of the Turkish Republic of Cyprus
28 Cockspur Street
London SW1Y 5BN
☎ 071 930 4853

As North Cyprus is not officially recognised by the international community there are no foreign embassies. Informal help can be given by the British High Commission.

Driving Documents and Regulations

South

Visitors are allowed to use their national driving licence or an international driving licence.

The Green Card insurance document is not accepted in Cyprus and so specific cover should be arranged either in advance or at the port of entry.

Car hire insurance tends not to cover the underside and tyres of the cars. Car hirers should also be aware that they may have to pay extra for a collision damage waiver otherwise they will be liable for up to the first CY£500 of any damage.

Many car hire companies do not hire to people under 21.

Driving is on the left.

Mopeds are for hire in most resorts. They tend to be hired out without crash helmets and visitors should take extreme care as many visitors are injured each year when driving mopeds.

North

The visitor's own national driving licence is all that is required. Specific insurance cover for those bringing their own cars should be arranged, the international Green Card is not valid in North Cyprus.

Driving is on the left.

Emergencies and Health

ILLNESS & INJURY
South

199 is the general emergency number for police and ambulance. General hospitals have casualty departments with good facilities for emergency cases. Medical services have to be paid for and so visitors should take out medical insurance.

Doctor's surgeries are open 9am-1pm and 4pm-7pm. Hotels will also arrange medical services.

Cyprus has a healthy climate and no vaccinations are required. There is no rabies. Mosquitos are a nuisance but not a health hazard and visitors should simply take insect repellent with them.

Hospitals:

Nicosia ☎ 02 45111
Limassol ☎ 05 330333
Larnaca ☎ 04 630311

Paphos ☎ 06 232364
Paralimni ☎ 03 821211
Polis ☎ 06 321431

North
Police:
Nicosia [Lefkosa] ☎ *020 71311*
Kyrenia [Girne] ☎ *081 52014*
Famagusta [Gazimagusa]
☎ *036 65310*

There are hospitals in Kyrenia [Girne] and Famagusta [Gazimagusa] and emergency facilities in all but the most remote areas. Visitors need take out their own holiday insurance.

First Aid:
Nicosia [Lefkosa] ☎ *020 71441*
Famagusta [Gazimagusa] ☎ *036 65310*
Kyrenia [Girne] ☎ *081 52014*
Morphou [Guzelyurt] ☎ *071 42140*
Lefka [Lefke] ☎ *078 17423*

CAR ACCIDENTS
Policemen usually speak English. Cypriots tend to be very highly strung in accidents and visitors should wait until a policeman arrives and take note of the details of the accident, perhaps by taking a photograph. Those hiring a car should ensure that the rate includes collision damage waiver (CDW) which will provide the equivalent of fully comprehensive cover.

BREAKDOWNS
The Cyprus Automobile Association, which is affiliated to its international counterparts, offers a breakdown service to its members.

Cyprus Automobile Association
12 Chr Mylonas Street
PO Box 2279
Nicosia 141
☎ 02 313233

Drivers of hire cars will be issued with instructions on what to do if their car breaks down, usually being given a telephone contact number.

North
There is no formal breakdown service. Hire car firms will inform clients of their own arrangements.

Entertainment and Festivals

While Cyprus is not a major centre for international culture many events are arranged during the summer. The municipal theatre in Nicosia has plays in English and Greek and there are performances of Classical drama in the Roman amphitheatre at *Kourion* and in the open-air amphitheatre at Larnaca.

There are also numerous festivals across the island at different times of year. These include:

Epiphany
Throwing the cross into the sea at coastal towns

Spring Carnival
Two weeks before Lent. The most famous festival takes place in Limassol but there are also celebrations in Larnaca and Paphos

Green Monday
First day of Lent. Picnics in the country

Processions of St Lazaro
30 March in Larnaca

Easter
Grand celebrations across the island

May
Flower festivals in Limassol, Larnaca, Paphos and Paralimni

Cataclysmos (Pentecost)
Festivals and folk dancing mainly in Larnaca but also in some other coastal towns

September
Limassol wine festival

Virtually all the towns have a programme of 'summer events' which include plays, music and exhibitions.

There are also festivals in the villages to celebrate saint's days or the end of the harvest. The tourist office publishes comprehensive information about all the above events throughout the summer.

The resorts offer their own entertainment ranging from discos to traditional dancing in the tavernas at which audience participation is usually expected.

Nicosia has several cinemas, some of which are open air. Limassol also has a few cinemas. The films are usually in English with Greek subtitles.

North
Children's Festival 23 April
Youth Festival 19 May
Turkish National Day 29 October
Turkish Cypriot National Day 15 November

Organised entertainment is much less prevalent in the north and tends to focus around the hotels and restaurants.

Essential Things to Take

South

Film for cameras is readily available but should not be bought from shops where it has been stored in the sun. Batteries for SLR cameras are not widely available. Although sun cream and insect repellent is widely available, it is wise to take your own .

In summer light clothes are all that are needed except for those staying in the mountains where it can be cool at night.

The electricty supply is 240 volts AC and most hotels are fitted for UK-style three pin plugs.

North

Supplies are less readily available as virtually everything has to be brought in from Turkey. However, most essential items can be obtained in the main towns although there may not be a wide choice. It is probably wise to bring films, sun cream and insect repellent from home.

Food and Drink

In all the resorts there is a multitude of restaurants offering a range of food, both Greek and European. Most meals in summer are taken outside, sometimes across a road, offering the entertaining sight of the waiters weaving between the traffic with the customer's order.

Specialist vegetarian food is difficult to find.

For sweets visitors may like to try the Greek cake shop which have a large array of cakes served with coffee and a glass of water. Ice cream shops also abound.

Greek Dishes
Mezedhes (meze): a collection of appetisers
Taramosalata: fish roe paste dip served as a starter
Tzatsiki: yoghurt and cucumber dip
Halloumi: traditional Cypriot cheese
Kebab: meat roasted on a skewer in pitta bread
Kleftiko: roast lamb cooked slowly in traditional ovens
Moussaka: mince, aubergines and cheese sauce
Stifado: stew of beef and tomato
Baklava: sweet pastry with nuts and cinammon
Kadeffi: stringy, sticky sweet pastry

Soujoukko: strings of nuts soaked in grape juice which then sets. This sweet is sold at village fairs in intimidating lengths.

Wine and Drink
Commandaria St John is a sweet dessert wine from Kolossi
Keo Hock, White Lady, Arsinoe and Aphrodite are local white wines
Othello and Afames are the best of the red wines
Keo and Carlsberg beer are made locally
Ouzo is a strong aniseed drink
The water is safe to drink.

Fruit is in plentiful supply both in the shops and from stalls at the side of the roads. While eating out is relatively cheap, self catering is another easy option. The supermarkets are good and well supplied.

Turkish Dishes
The diet of the Turkish Cypriots is broadly similar to that of the Greek Cypriots although some of the dishes may have different names.
In the north there are a few local wines; Kantara white and red are two examples but the wine industry is still in its infancy.

Language and Road Signs

Greek is the official language of the south although almost everybody speaks very good English and it is only in the mountain villages that a knowledge of Greek will be useful. The Cypriots are less proficient in their command of written English and menus can range from the incomprehensible to the comical.

Road signs are in both Greek and English characters. There has been a recent move to alter these translations to make them more phonetic, hence Larnaca is now becoming Larnaka, Agia instead of Ayia and one or two more significant changes: *Khirokitia* has changed to *Choirokoitia*. This book uses the form most widely seen on official signs. Although the tourist offices provide very good free plans of the major resorts and the surrounding areas, the placenames are often spelt differently to those on road signs. Note that 'y' and 'g' are used interchangebly.

Visitors should also note that many villages may have the same or similar names. There are numerous variations of Ayios, Ayia, Ayii depending on the gender of the saint. Villages are often in two halves, Kato (Upper) and Pano (lower).

North

A knowledge of English is less widespread and some knowledge of Turkish could help. There are also problems in the fact that signs have Turkish names for places better known for their Greek names and maps are not always consistent so it is essential to have a map with the Turkish names marked on it. In this book the Greek name is given, followed by the Turkish name in italics.

Legal Advice

Cypriot law is broadly similar to that in Britain. Visitors are only likely to encounter problems if they stray near miltary areas. In case of legal difficulties visitors should contact their embassy or consulate. See under Documents for addresses.

North

As the north is not officially recognised there is no diplomatic representation. A representative of the British High Comission travels to North Nicosia every weekday morning and works in the old British High Commission.

Media and Newspapers

There are ten daily newspapers, nine in Greek and one in English, these includes two evening papers. There are also four weekly papers. All the papers have clear political affiliations across the whole spectrum. The *Cyprus Mail* (daily) and *The Cyprus Weekly* are in English. Newspapers from Britain are widely available a day late.

Visitors with a radio will also be able to pick up BFBS (British Forces Broadcasting Service) which carries many BBC Radio 4 programmes. There is also a programme for tourists broadcast in English on Channel 1 (FM 97.2MHz) which gives weather forecasts and ideas of what to do.

North

The north has its own Cyprus Times *which is an English weekly.*

Miscellaneous Information
DRESS REGULATIONS

Visitors should not wear shorts or have bare shoulders if they wish to visit churches and monasteries. Visitors will have to remove their shoes to enter mosques.

POST

Stamps: postcards to Europe 16 cents, to US 18 cents, to Australia 23 cents. Stamps are available from post offices, newspaper kiosks and hotels.

Post Offices are open Mon-Sat 7.30am-1.pm (1.30pm in winter). A few offices are open in the afternoon.

North

Post Offices are open Mon-Fri 8am-1pm and 2pm-4pm, Sat 8.30am-12.30pm. All post goes via Turkey.

POLITICAL AFFAIRS

Obviously the division of the island is a continuing controversy and sensitivities on both sides are extremely acute. Photography near military camps is forbidden.

RELIGION

The religion of the south is Greek Orthodox and is still very important. There are churches in almost every village on the island and the black clad, bearded priest is very much the centre of the village. There is less of a division between the secular and the religious in Cyprus than visitors may be used to. Indeed political activity has been centred round the church for hundreds of years, culminating in the Archbishop Makarios becoming President.

North

The Turks are Muslim but not fervent about religion.

PETS

Dogs are controlled because they carry a parasite transmitted from sheep. There are, however, huge numbers of cats everywhere on the island. Pets brought to the island have to be placed in quarantine.

TIPPING

Service is included in bills. Although tips are always appreciated they are not expected as a matter of course, except perhaps by taxi drivers in the south.

DISABLED VISITORS

Facilities for disabled people are generally poor with steps and poorly maintained pavements posing the main problems. Ayia Napa and Paphos are the only resorts with hills. If informed in advance the airports provide facilities for those in wheelchairs.

Travel agents and groups for the disabled in the visitor's home country will have more detailed information on specific facilities. The tourist office also issues a leaflet giving advice to travellers with disabilities.

Opening Times

In both north and south opening times vary between summer and winter. Summer times apply from 1 May to 30 September.

South

These times may vary in major resorts where shops will stay open later in the evenings, although all are still likely to have a siesta period. Half day closing is Wednesday.

Summer:
Shops/offices Mon, Tues, Thurs, Fri 8am-1pm, 4-7pm; Wed, Sat 8am-1pm
Banks 8.15am-12 noon
Post Offices Mon-Sat 7.30am-1pm. Some offices open in the afternoon.
Public services Mon-Sat 7.30am-1.30pm

Winter:
Shops/offices Mon, Tues, Thurs, Fri 8am-1pm, 2.30- 5.30pm; Wed, Sat 8am-1pm
Public Services Mon-Fri 7.30am-2pm; Sat 7.30am-1pm

North

Summer:
Shops 7.30am-1pm, 4-6pm
Banks Mon-Sat 8am-12 noon
Offices Mon-Fri 7.30am-2pm
Post Offices 8am-1pm, 2-5pm
Museums and archaeological sites 9am-1.30pm, 4.30-6.30pm

Winter:
Shops 8am-1pm, 2-6pm
Offices Mon-Fri 8am-1pm, 2-5pm
Museums and archaeological sites 8am-1.00pm, 2.30pm-5pm
Museums are open Tuesday to Saturday, winter and summer.

Public Holidays

South

New Year's Day

6th January
Epiphany

Green Monday
Also known as Clean Monday, 50 days before Greek Easter

25 March
Greek National Day, a major religious holiday with processions in town

1 April
Greek Cypriot National Day

Good Friday, Easter Sunday, Easter Monday (variable)
Easter is very important in the Greek calendar with mass on Good Friday followed by processions. There are firework displays on Saturday night and on Sunday the traditional pastime of breaking coloured eggs.

1 May
Labour Day

15 August
Dormition of the Virgin Mary

1 October
Cyprus Independence Day

28 October
Ochi Day, celebrates the Greek refusal to let Mussolini pass through Greece in 1940 (*ochi* means 'no'). This is marked by parades and waving of the Greek flag.

Christmas Day

Boxing Day

All shops and public offices are closed on public holidays with the exception of those in major resorts. The major archaeological sites and museums remain open.

North

The Muslim holidays, Ramadan and Kurban Bayram vary each year.

Public Holidays

1 Jan	*1, 30 August*
23, 26, 27, 28 April	*11, 29 October*
1, 19 May	*15 November*
4-7, 20 July	

Personal Insurance

As medical treatment has to be paid for it is strongly recommended that visitors take out medical insurance. No innoculations are required. Basic medical supplies are easily available, although those with specific medical requirements should check availability in advance and take their prescriptions with them.

Shopping

Nicosia and Limassol have the widest range of shops. Local handicrafts are widely available. There is some fine pottery available including replicas of the terracotta figurines from Cyprus's prehistory. The villages of Phini and Kornos are particularly well known for their pottery. Fine basketwork is on sale in many of the villages in eastern Cyprus near Ayia Napa.

The copper industry is less important to Cyprus these days than in its ancient past, but metalwork continues both in copper and silver with some fine jewellery on sale.

Lefkara is famous for its lace and lace making is a popular pastime for Cypriot women, both in the villages and the towns. Leather goods, bags and shoes in particular are very good value.

These goods are available in all the tourist areas as well as from the Cyprus Handicraft service which has shops in Nicosia, Limassol, Larnaca and Paphos.

Cyprus, surprisingly, is known for its low-cost spectacles and it may be worth taking a prescription on holiday to acquire a new pair of glasses.

Hand-made suits can be made by tailors found in the narrow streets of Nicosia and Limassol and especially in the north where individual traditional service is still possible.

Cyprus Delight (Turkish Delight) is made in Yersokipos near Paphos.

Visitors will also see an enormous number of pirate video tapes on sale, if they wish to participate in this trade they should make sure that they check the quality of the tapes before buying. In particular check beyond the first five minutes.

North
Rugs and copperware are good buys in the North, as is pottery which is on sale in all the towns.

Sports

There are numerous opportunities for sports lovers in Cyprus, both as participants and spectators. For precise details, see Additional Information sections for each region.

Boats

Visitors can hire speed boats all long the coast or take boat trips. (For details see individual chapters).

Cycling

Bicycles and mopeds can be hired at many of the resorts although the heat of summer may prove a deterrent to any energetic cycling.

Cyprus Cycling Federation
PO Box 8126
Nicosia
☎ 02 450875

Diving and Fishing

Snorkelling is easy at the main resorts. Spear fishing is only allowed with a licence. This and licences for angling in dams are obtainable from the District Fisheries Department:

Nicosia ☎ 02 403527
Limassol ☎ 05 330470
Larnaca ☎ 04 630294
Paphos ☎ 06 240268

Sailing

There are sailing clubs at Limassol, Larnaca, Paphos and Kyrenia. Dinghies can be hired at the main resorts.

Skiing

Skiing takes place on Mount Olympus between January and March. See the Troodos chapter for further information.

Cyprus Ski Federation
PO Box 2185
Nicosia
☎ 02 365340

Walking

The summer heat makes energetic walking unpleasant, but outside July and August there are plenty of opportunities to explore the island on foot. The tourist office have also set up some marked trails around Troodos village. There are also trails in the Akamas peninsula and at Cape Greco. In the North there may be problems of access because of military areas.

Watersports

Swimming is of course popular throughout the island. There are beaches run by the tourist office near the major towns, but plenty of other places to swim all along the coast. There are facilities for windsurfing and waterskiing at the resorts.

Waterskiing conditions are best in the early morning and evening. There are opportunities to swim at the Eleon and new Olympic pools in Nicosia where day membership is possible.

Spectator Sports
The Cyprus Motor Rally in September starts from Nicosia and then runs through the mountains.

International football matches which take place in Nicosia and Limassol. The Cyprus League plays from October to May.

There is a horse racing track just outside Nicosia near St Paul's Street.

Telephones

Cyprus is connected by international direct dialling to ninety-five countries. There are numerous coin operated telephone boxes . Coins of 2, 10, 20 cents can be used. There are also some telephones which take phone cards of CY£2 or CY£5.

Dialling Codes
UK 0044
USA 001
192 for the operator
194 for international operator

Local Codes
Local codes have recently changed and visitors may occasionally see the old 3-figure versions

Nicosia 02
Limassol 05
Larnaca 04
Paphos 06
Ayia Napa 03

Paralimni 03
Platres 05
Polis 06

North
There are distinctive red phone boxes in the main towns.

Local Codes
Nicosia [Lefkosa] *020*
Famagusta [Gazimagusa] *036*
Kyrenia [Girne] *081*
Morphou [Guzelyurt] *071*
Lefke [Lefka] *078*
Y Iskele [Trikomon] *037*
Lapta [Lapithos] *082*
Karavostasi [Gemikonagi] *077*

Theft

There is very little crime in Cyprus with other tourists more of a problem than the Cypriots themselves. If something is stolen contact the police . Most policemen speak English.

Toilets

Toilets are good in hotels and there are plenty of public toilets at the main sites visited by tourists. They are usually clean, at the beginning of the day at least. Due to the plumbing system toilet paper cannot be flushed but has to be put in the waste paper basket by the WC.

Travel

AIR

Most travellers arrive by air. Over thirty airlines operate services to Cyprus. The national carrier is Cyprus Airways which operates scheduled flights.

Cyprus Airways
21 Alkaeus Street
PO Box 1903
Nicosia
☎ 02 443054

also
50 Archbishop Makarios Ave
Nicosia
☎ 02 441966

There are two international airports (the former international airport in Nicosia is under UN control and not in use), Larnaca and Paphos.

Larnaca Airport
6km (4miles) from Larnaca town centre
53km (33 miles) from Nicosia
76km (47 miles) from Limassol
53km (33 miles) from Ayia Napa
150 km (93 miles) from Paphos

Facilities: Tourist Information (24 hours) and hotel reservation service. Foreign Exchange. Duty free shops. Cafés. Car hire. Facilities for disabled travellers. Post Office. Car Park

Paphos Airport
13km (8 miles) east of Paphos town centre
72km (45 miles) from Limassol
127km (86 miles)from Larnaca
179km (112 miles) from Ayia Napa
147km (92 miles) from Nicosia

Facilities: Tourist information. Foreign exchange. Duty free shop. Café. Paphos airport is very small and these facilities can get very crowded. Visitors should not expect an extensive choice in the shops or cafés.

Both airports can be crowded and uncomfortable in summer. Package tourists will be met at the airport. Others can take taxis. All the major hire car companies are represented at the airports.

Flight Times:
from London 4½ hours
from Athens 1hr 40 minutes
from Paris 3½ hours

North
There are no direct flights to the North, all come via Turkey. Flights arrive at Ercan Airport 23 miles (37km) from Kyrenia, 9 miles (15km) from Nicosia and 30 miles (48km) from Famagusta. The airport is reasonably good.

SEA
There are ferry services from Piraeus (Greece), Rhodes, Haifa (Israel) and Port Said (Egypt). As they stop off en route, the journey takes two days. Most ships arrive at Limassol, with a few services from Larnaca. Most only run in spring and summer. At the ports there is a tourist information office, exchange facilities, duty free shops, cafés and a car insurance office. Comprehensive information is available from a tourist office leaflet.

Main shipping operators:

Salamis Tours
Limassol ☎ 05 355555
From Piraues via Iraklion and Rhodes

Sol Maritime Ltd
1 Irene St
Limassol ☎ 05 357000
From Piraeus via Rhodes and terminating in Haifa

Stability Line
38 Olympiou Street
Limassol
☎ 05 343978
From Piraeus via Iraklion, Rhodes and terminating in Haifa. Also services to Rhodes, Mykonos, Piraeus, Corfu.

For visitors with a few days to spare there are 2-3 day cruises to the Holy Land and/or Egypt from Limassol, with transfers from the main resorts:

Louis Cruise Lines
158 Franklin Roosvelt Ave
Limassol
☎ 05 346304/358660/350947

There is also a service to Larnaca from Jounieh in Lebanon.

North

A daily ferry runs from Kyrenia [Girne] *to Tasucu and Mersin in Turkey which takes 6 hours. A car ferry service goes from Famagusta* [Gazimagusa] *to Mersin.*

Turkish Maritime lines
Turk Bankasi Ltd
☎ *03 665494*

PUBLIC TRANSPORT

There are numerous bus companies offering different services (see regional chapters). Information available at tourist offices.

An alternative way to travel is by service taxi which travel from all the major towns on the island. Seats can be booked by phone. They are shared between 4-7 people. Private taxis are also available and reasonably good value.

CAR HIRE

Car hire companies do not usually hire to people under 21. Hired cars are known as Z cars because their number plates are marked by a Z. There are car hire firms all around the island and at the airports. Car hire is relatively expensive, a seemingly cheap rate may not include a collision damage waiver, without which the driver is responsible for the first CY£300-500 of any damage.

DRIVING

Traffic drives on the left.

Speed limits:
Motorway (Nicosia-Limassol) 100km/h (60mph)
Other roads 60 km/h (40mph)
In towns 50km/h (30mph)

Seat belts are compulsory for front seat passengers and childen under 5 cannot travel in the front. Children between the ages of 5 and 10 in the front seat have to have a child's seat belt.

Rush hour in towns is 7.30-8am, 1-1.30pm and 5-6pm, later in summer.

It can be dangerous driving west into the sunset, especially on mountain roads. In summer it is very dusty and drivers should make sure that their screen wash is topped up.

Roads are of reasonable quality especially the new major highways. Dirt tracks are usually passable, although care is always needed and progress will be much slower than on tarred roads. The roads in the villages can be very poor and it is easy for the unwary to become lost.

It should be remembered that Cypriot drivers are reckless and tend to ignore road rules; passing through lights at red, driving in the middle of the road and overtaking without indicating are common occurrences.

Drivers should note that cars can become very hot if they are parked in the sun and where possible should be parked in the shade. Cameras should not be left in parked cars or the film may deteriorate.

FUEL

Filling stations are open Mon-Fri 6am-6pm, Sat and Sun 6am-4pm

On Sundays only certain petrol stations are open and it is unwise to leave refilling until Sunday.

There are very few self-service stations. Few accept credit cards. Almost all hire cars take the petrol marked Super.

There are few filling stations outside the main towns. For instance the nearest filling stations for most of the west of Cyprus is in Paphos, and even there they are mainly grouped along the road to Polis in the upper town. Do not venture on a long trip or to the Troodos Mountains without a full fuel tank.

North

Traffic also drives on the left in the north, although some car hire firms have left-hand drive cars. Even the tourist office warn of the low standard of driving.

There is a speed limit of 30mph in towns.

Most fuel stations close at 7pm and very few are open on Sundays. It is important to fill up before going to remote areas like the Karpas.

Tourist Offices in Cyprus and Abroad

Cyprus
Laiki Yitonia
(East of Elfetheria Square)
Nicosia
☎ 02 444264

15 Spyros Araouzos Street
Limassol
☎ 05 362756

35 George A St
Potamos tis Yermosoyias
(opposite Dhassoudi beach)
Limassol
☎ 05 323211

Limassol Harbour
☎ 05 343868

Democratias Square
Larnaca
☎ 04 654322

Larnaca Airport
(open 24 hours)
☎ 04 654389

3 Gladstone Street
Paphos
☎ 06 232841

Paphos airport
(service to all flights)
☎ 06 236833

17 Archbishop Makarios Ave
Ayia Napa
☎ 03 721796

Platres
☎ 05 421316
Open: April-October

Abroad
213 Regent Street
London W1R 8DA
United Kingdom
☎ 071 734 9822

13 East 40th Street
New York 10016
☎ 212 6835280
USA

North
*The tourist offices are less well
organised in the north.*

Nicosia [Lefkosa]
☎ *020 75051*
Just outside town on Girne road

*There is also an unofficial tourist
office in Kumarcilar Khan*

Kyrenia [Girne]
*Fehmi Ercan Cad
(200yd from Dorana Hotel)*
☎ *081 52145*

Famagusta [Gazimagusa]
*Fevzi Cakmak Bulvari
(by the Monument of Victory)*
☎ *036 62864*

*UK
North Cyprus Tourist Office
28 Cockspur Street
London SW1Y 5BN*
☎ *071 930 4853*

Nicosia	**Distance in South Cyprus** miles with km in brackets					
50 (80)	Limassol					
95 (152)	45 (72)	Paphos				
32 (51)	44 (70)	89 (142)	Larnaca			
50 (80)	32 (51)	77 (123)	76 (121)	Troodos		
54 (86)	70 (112)	115 (184)	26 (41)	102 (163)	Ayia Napa	
118 (188)	68 (108)	23 (37)	112 (177)	100 (160)	138 (220)	Polis

Nicosia [Lefkosa]	**Distance in North Cyprus** miles with km in brackets			
16 (26)	Kyrenia [Girne]			
38 (61)	45 (72)	Famagusta [Gazimagusta]		
25 (40)	44 (70)	59 (94)	Morphou [Guzelyurt]	
15 (24)	23 (37)	32 (51)	36 (58)	Ercan (airport)

INDEX

MPC

A Note to the Reader

Thank you for buying this book, we hope it has helped you to plan and enjoy your visit. We have worked hard to produce a guidebook which is as accurate as possible. With this in mind, any comments, suggestions or useful information you may have would be appreciated.

Please send your letters to:

The Editor
Moorland Publishing Co Ltd
Moor Farm Road West
Ashbourne
Derbyshire
DE6 1HD

The Travel Specialists

Visitor's Guides
Tour & Explore with MPC Visitor's Guides

Austria
Austria: Tyrol &
  Vorarlberg
Britain:
Cornwall & Isles of
  Scilly
Cotswolds
Devon
East Anglia
Guernsey, Alderney
  and Sark
Hampshire & Isle of
  Wight
Denmark
Jersey
Kent
Lake District
Scotland: Lowlands
Somerset, Dorset &
  Wiltshire
North Wales and
  Snowdonia
North York Moors,
  York & Coast
Northumbria
Northern Ireland
Peak District
Sussex
Yorkshire Dales &
  North Pennines

Crete
Cyprus
Egypt
Finland
Florida
France:
Alps & Jura
Corsica
Dordogne
Loire
Massif Central
Normandy Landing
  Beaches
Provence & Côte
  d'Azur
Germany:
Bavaria
Black Forest
Rhine & Mosel
Southern Germany
Northern Germany
Iceland
Italy:
Florence & Tuscany
Italian Lakes
Northern Italy
Mauritius,
  Rodrigues &
  Reunion
Peru

Spain:
Costa Brava to Costa
  Blanca
Mallorca, Menorca,
  Ibiza &
  Formentera
Northern & Central
  Spain
Southern Spain &
  Costa del Sol
Sweden
Switzerland
Tenerife
Turkey
Yugoslavia: The
  Adriatic Coast

World Traveller
*The new larger format
Visitor's Guides*

Belgium & Luxem-
  bourg
Czechoslovakia
France
Holland
Norway
Portugal
USA

MPC Guides
Explore the World with the Best in Travel Guides

Off the Beaten Track
Austria
Britain
France
Greece
Italy
Portugal
Scandinavia
Spain
Switzerland
West Germany

Spectrum Guides
African Wildlife Safaris
Kenya
Maldives
Pakistan
Seychelles
Tanzania
Zimbabwe

Insider's Guides
Australia
Bali
California
Eastern Canada
Western Canada
China
Florida
Hawaii
Hong Kong
India
Indonesia
Japan
Kenya
Malaysia & Singapore
Mexico
Nepal
New England
Spain
Thailand
Turkey
Russia

A complete catalogue of all our travel guides to over 125 destinations is available on request